Legendary Football Quarterbacks

Legendary Football Quarterbacks

Other books in the History Makers series:

America's Founders

Artists of the Renaissance

Astronauts

Baseball Greats

Cartoonists

Civil War Generals of the Confederacy

Civil War Generals of the Union

Cult Leaders

Dictators

Disease Detectives

Fighters Against American Slavery

Gangsters

Great Authors of Children's Literature

Great Composers

Great Conquerors

Great Male Comedians

Great Women Comedians

Gunfighters

Heroes of the Holocaust

Hitler's Henchmen

Home Run Kings

Influential First Ladies

The Kennedys

Leaders of Ancient Greece

Leaders of Black Civil Rights

Leaders of Women's Suffrage

Magicians and Illusionists

Male Olympic Champions

Medieval Knights and Warriors

Native American Chiefs and Warriors

Pioneers of the American West

Pioneers of the Internet

Pirates

Polar Explorers

Presidential Assassins

Presidents and Scandals

Rock and Roll Legends

Rulers of Ancient Egypt

Rulers of Ancient Rome

Scientists of Ancient Greece

Serial Killers

Spies

Twentieth-Century American Writers

Women Inventors

Women Leaders of Nations

Women of the American Revolution

Women Olympic Champions

Women Pop Stars

Legendary
Football
Quarterbacks

By John F. Grabowski

**LUCENT
BOOKS**®

THOMSON
™
GALE

San Diego • Detroit • New York • San Francisco • Cleveland
New Haven, Conn. • Waterville, Maine • London • Munich

On Cover: (clockwise from center) Joe Namath, Sammy Baugh, Joe Montana, Otto Graham, Johnny Unitas

TH BA

LIBRARY OF CONGRESS CATALOGING-IN-PUBLICATION DATA

Grabowski, John F.
  Legendary football quarterbacks / by John F. Grabowski.
p. cm. — (History makers)
Summary: Profiles some of the top-rated quarterbacks of all time, including Sammy
Baugh, Otto Graham, Johnny Unitas, Fran Tarkenton, Joe Namath, Joe Montana, and
Dan Marino.
Includes bibliographical references and index.
  ISBN 1-59018-230-8 (alk. paper)
  1. Quarterbacks (Football)—United States—Biography—Juvenile literature. 2.
Quarterbacks (Football)—Rating of—United States—Juvenile literature. [1. Football
players.] I. Title. II. Series
  GV939.H1G72 2003
  796.332'0921'2—dc21
                                                                    2002156786

CONTENTS

FOREWORD

The literary form most often referred to as "multiple biography" was perfected in the first century A.D. by Plutarch, a perceptive and talented moralist and historian who hailed from the small town of Chaeronea in central Greece. His most famous work, *Parallel Lives*, consists of a long series of biographies of noteworthy ancient Greek and Roman statesmen and military leaders. Frequently, Plutarch compares a famous Greek to a famous Roman, pointing out similarities in personality and achievements. These expertly constructed and very readable tracts provided later historians and others, including playwrights like Shakespeare, with priceless information about prominent ancient personages and also inspired new generations of writers to tackle the multiple biography genre.

The Lucent History Makers series proudly carries on the venerable tradition handed down from Plutarch. Each volume in the series consists of a set of five to eight biographies of important and influential historical figures who are linked together by a common factor. In *Rulers of Ancient Rome*, for example, all the figures were generals, consuls, or emperors of either the Roman Republic or Empire; while the subjects of *Fighters Against American Slavery*, though they lived in different places and times, all shared the same goal, namely the eradication of human servitude. Mindful that politicians and military leaders are not (and never have been) the only people who shape the course of history, the editors of the series have also included representatives from a wide range of endeavors, including scientists, artists, writers, philosophers, religious leaders, and sports figures.

Each book is intended to give a range of figures—some well known, others less known; some who made a great impact on history, others who made only a small impact. For instance, by making Columbus's initial voyage possible, Spain's Queen Isabella I, featured in *Women Leaders of Nations*, helped to open up the New World to exploration and exploitation by the European powers. Unarguably, therefore, she made a major contribution to a series of events that had momentous consequences for the entire world. By contrast, Catherine II, the eighteenth-century Russian queen, and Golda Meir, the modern Israeli prime minister, did not play roles of global impact; however, their policies and actions significantly influenced the historical development of both their own countries and their regional neighbors. Regardless of their relative importance in the greater historical scheme, all of the figures chronicled in the History Makers series made contributions to posterity; and their public achievements, as well as what is known about their private lives, are presented and evaluated in light of the most recent scholarship.

In addition, each volume in the series is documented and substantiated by a wide array of primary and secondary source quotations. The primary source quotes enliven the text by presenting eyewitness views of the times and culture in which each history maker lived; while the secondary source quotes, taken from the works of respected modern scholars, offer expert elaboration and/ or critical commentary. Each quote is footnoted, demonstrating to the reader exactly where biographers find their information. The footnotes also provide the reader with the means of conducting additional research. Finally, to further guide and illuminate readers, each volume in the series features photographs, two bibliographies, and a comprehensive index.

The History Makers series provides both students engaged in research and more casual readers with informative, enlightening, and entertaining overviews of individuals from a variety of circumstances, professions, and backgrounds. No doubt all of them, whether loved or hated, benevolent or cruel, constructive or destructive, will remain endlessly fascinating to each new generation seeking to identify the forces that shaped their world.

The Toughest Position in Sports

Indianapolis Colts star quarterback Peyton Manning once said:

> The toughest position in sports is sort of a bar discussion that can never be solved. But I don't see how it's not quarterback. Point guard [in basketball] is tough, but those guys don't have to deal with crowd noise. Golfers work in silence, pretty much. A pitcher might have a line drive hit back at him, but that's his biggest fear, and it doesn't happen that much. A quarterback can't hear, he's calling a lot of plays at the line, he's got five or six good athletes bigger than he is coming at him every play, and it wears on you to get hit, get hit, get hit, and have to come back and make a play. And you have to make the right decision. One bad throw can lose a game.[1]

It takes a special kind of athlete to do the quarterback's job well. The position requires, among other things, better than average physical skills, intelligence, fearlessness, and the ability to lead. Over the years, approximately eight hundred men have attempted the task at the elite levels of pro football. Only a handful of those have risen to the very top of their profession.

The Making of a Great Quarterback

Observers have long debated what sets a great quarterback apart from the other members of his trade. One criterion many have used to award a player legendary status is statistical superiority in a particular category. For example, the fact that San Francisco 49er Steve Young had the highest quarterback passer rating in history makes him qualify as a legend in the eyes of many people. (The quarterback passer rating is determined by a complex formula based on passes attempted, completions, passing yardage, touchdown passes, and interceptions. As of the start of the 2002 season, Young's mark of 96.8 is the NFL career best. At 92.3,

San Francisco 49ers quarterback Steve Young in action. Young has one of the highest quarterback passer ratings in history and is recognized as a football legend.

Young's former teammate Joe Montana is the only other player with a mark above 90.)

Yet statistics can often be deceiving. Former Seattle Seahawk Dave Krieg ranks number twenty on the passer list with a rating of 81.5. This statistical ranking places Krieg ahead of such Hall of Famers as Bart Starr, Fran Tarkenton, Dan Fouts, Johnny Unitas, Bob Griese, Sid Luckman, Terry Bradshaw, and Joe Namath. Krieg, however, is rarely mentioned as a candidate for football's Hall of Fame.

Physical Attributes

Although excellent passing statistics do not necessarily correlate with physical strength, the ability to throw a long pass is still a much sought-after attribute in a quarterback. However, only a few men have gained legendary status on the strength of their arms. The powerful rocket arm of John Elway led the Denver Broncos to a pair of Super Bowl victories while giving opposing cornerbacks and safeties nightmares.

The ability to throw a bomb does not guarantee legendary status. Arguably the strongest arm of all time belonged to a player who was little more than a journeyman, Rudy Bukich, who played sixteen years in the NFL in the 1950s and 1960s. In only two of those seasons, however, did Bukich complete as many as one hundred passes. Football insiders remember him rather as the man who once threw a ball one hundred yards in practice. As Hall of Fame end Mike Ditka related, "It's true. I saw Rudy do it. I was on the field that day. Now, I'd seen him try it before, and it'd go maybe 95. But he did throw it 100 that one time."[2]

The Importance of Intangibles

Although arm strength is the quality that draws oohs and aahs from the fans, there are intangibles that are perhaps even more important in the makeup of an outstanding quarterback. Character traits like leadership, toughness, and the ability to perform under pressure are things that cannot be quantified as yards per pass can be. Virtues like these often make the difference between winning and losing.

Some observers might even argue that winning itself is the best measure of greatness. Using winning as a guideline, Bart Starr and Terry Bradshaw stand among the immortals on the basis of leading their clubs to victories in the Super Bowl. On the other hand, winning football's ultimate game was not enough to raise Jeff Hostetler of the New York Giants or Trent Dilfer of the Baltimore Ravens to the same level.

Historical Significance

Sometimes, excelling is less important than simply being innovative. Being the first one to do—or be—something is sometimes reason enough to bring a quarterback everlasting fame. For example, part of Sid Luckman's reputation is based on his being the first great T formation quarterback in the National Football League (NFL). Again, however, such moments do not automatically insure immortality. Despite being the first quarterback to have a four-hundred-yard passing game and one-hundred-yard rushing game in the same season, Jeff Blake's career statistics are such that he will never be enshrined with his sport's greater luminaries in the hallowed halls of the Professional Football Hall of Fame in Canton, Ohio.

The Greatest of the Great

Undeniably, however, some men do qualify as legends for standing out in these categories. Sammy Baugh is credited with making

Hall of Fame Quarterbacks

Name	Years	Name	Years
Sammy Baugh	1937–1952	Bobby Lane	1948–1962
George Blanda	1949–1975	Sid Luckman	1939–1950
Terry Bradshaw	1970–1983	Joe Montana	1979–1994
Earl Clark	1931–1938	Joe Namath	1965–1977
Jimmy Conzelman	1920–1929	Clarence Parker	1937–1946
Len Dawson	1957–1975	Bart Starr	1956–1971
John Driscoll	1919–1929	Roger Staubach	1969–1979
Dan Fouts	1973–1987	Fran Tarkenton	1961–1978
Otto Graham	1946–1955	Y.A. Tittle	1948–1964
Bob Griese	1967–1980	Johnny Unitas	1956–1973
Arnie Herber	1930–1945	Norm Van Brocklin	1949–1960
Sonny Jurgensen	1957–1974	Bob Waterfield	1945–1952
Jim Kelly	1986–1996		

the forward pass an integral part of the pro football offense; Otto Graham is the sport's ultimate winner, having led his teams to the championship game ten consecutive seasons; Johnny Unitas's toughness cannot be measured by numbers, but was definitely part of the reason he was able to lead the Colts to two championships, including the overtime victory in the 1958 NFL Championship Game, credited with being the contest that helped bring professional football into the national spotlight; Fran Tarkenton was the first of pro football's scrambling quarterbacks; Joe Namath gave the American Football League (AFL) its first Super Bowl victory, an event that ultimately quickened the league's merger with the older, established NFL; Joe Montana is the only man to lead a team to four Super Bowl victories; and Dan Marino is the career leader in most passing categories.

Future years will undoubtedly see other quarterbacks perform heroic deeds and reach mythic status in the NFL. Included among them may be current stars such as Peyton Manning, Michael Vick, Steve McNair, Donovan McNabb, and Jeff Garcia. No one can deny, however, that the seven men whose lives are detailed in this book will retain their standing as legendary quarterbacks of the NFL.

CHAPTER 1

Sammy Baugh: The Revolutionary

With his powerful arm and whiplike throwing motion, "Slingin'" Sammy Baugh revolutionized the passing game in professional football. Yet Baugh was much more than simply the first man to make the forward pass a regular part of his arsenal. In addition to his skills as a quarterback, he was also a talented tailback, an excellent defensive back, and a superb punter. Because of this, many consider him to have been the best all-around player in the history of the game.

Deep in the Heart of Texas

Samuel Adrian Baugh was born on March 17, 1914, on a farm in the town of Temple, Texas, about halfway between Austin and Waco. His father worked for the Santa Fe Railroad, which had been instrumental in founding the town back in 1881. Sammy was a hard worker who did his best at everything he tried. This determination helped him excel in all sports.

The family lived in Temple until Sammy was sixteen and his father was transferred to Sweetwater, Texas. At Sweetwater High School, Sammy was a three-sport star, playing baseball, basketball, and football. His best sport was baseball, where the skinny youngster was a rifle-armed third baseman.

Baugh's arm was also a weapon in his position as tailback on the school's football team. (Back in the 1930s, the passing game was in its infancy. The tailback usually received the snap from center and initiated a passing or running play.) Baugh practiced for hours on end in order to hone his skills. In one of his exercises, he suspended an old tire from a rope attached to the limb of a tree in his yard. He swung the tire in a long arc, pendulum style, then repeatedly tried to throw the ball through the moving tire.

Baugh also practiced punting. Special teams were unheard of in those days, and most players performed on both offense and defense. Punting chores often went to the players who most handled the ball. "I worked at punting more than a lot of people do," he recalled. "I worked at it from high school. I'd go out on the football field where I wouldn't have anyone to kick to, and I'd stand on the 50-yard line and kick to spots on the field."[3]

A Two-Sport Star

Baugh's football skills improved at a rapid rate, but his future still seemed to lie in baseball. "Everybody thought I was a better baseball player growing up," he remembered. "I thought I was going to be a big-league baseball player."[4] It was while playing baseball with an Abilene semipro team called the Oilers that Baugh caught the eye of Leo "Dutch" Meyer, Texas Christian University's (TCU) baseball coach. Meyer was interested in Baugh not just because of his obvious skills on the baseball diamond, but because he had heard that he was also a star on both the football field and the basketball court. Meyer asked Baugh if he would be interested in attending TCU.

After graduating from Sweetwater, Baugh accepted a baseball scholarship and went to Fort Worth, where TCU was located. There, the six-foot-two-inch, 180-pound Baugh sparkled as a third baseman. In Baugh's junior year of 1934–1935, sportswriter Flem Hall bestowed upon him the nickname "Slingin' Sammy" because of his hard throws to first base.

In 1934, Meyer took over as the school's football coach. He invited Baugh to try out for the team. The youngster did so and soon earned a starting position. Baugh was introduced to Coach Meyer's spread offense, a formation that today would resemble the shotgun. The idea behind the spread offense was to help sustain offensive drives by interspersing running plays with passing plays. "We were sitting in a classroom trying to make sense out of writing on a blackboard," recalled Baugh. "Dutch comes in and says, 'We're going to be playing teams that can score on us every time they have the ball. The only way we can match them is to keep the ball away from them. And we're going to do it with short passing.'"[5]

As quarterback, defensive back, and punter, Baugh helped the Horned Frogs to an 11-1 record in his junior year. Their only loss was to undefeated Southern Methodist University by a score of 20-14, and in that game Baugh was sidelined with an injury. He then led them into the Sugar Bowl, where he rushed for 52 yards, punted for an average of 44.6 yards, and intercepted a pair of passes as TCU defeated Louisiana State University in a defensive duel and won by a score of 3-2.

Sammy Baugh originally played college baseball. He began to play football in his sophomore year and quickly established himself as a dominant player.

Although the Horned Frogs dropped to an 8-2-2 record in his senior year, Baugh compiled even more impressive statistics for himself. He completed just over 50 percent of his pass attempts, threw for a total of 1,261 yards, and logged ten touchdown passes. His average of 43 yards per punt was one of the highest in the country.

Baugh's three years at TCU were exceptional for a time when the running play was king. Baugh completed 270 of 587 pass attempts for 3,384 yards and 39 touchdowns. In addition to his play at quarterback, Baugh also averaged 40.9 yards on 198 punts, 12.4 yards on 80 punt returns, and 15.3 yards on 10 interceptions.

Sammy Baugh played as quarterback, defensive back, and punter for Texas Christian University.

On to the Pros

After his graduation from TCU, Baugh was selected by the Boston Redskins in the first round of the 1937 NFL draft. Baugh, however, was reluctant to accept Boston's offer. The pros played a plodding, slow-moving, defensive brand of football, which was not particularly fun to watch. Only five teams scored more than thirty points in a game in 1936, while fifteen contests ended in shutouts. Moreover, pro football was less than a thriving enterprise; teams could (and did) go bankrupt, so a player's financial security was at risk.

Baugh also hesitated because pro football was virtually unknown in the South, so the whole idea was therefore somewhat intimidating. "Down in Texas," recalled Baugh, "no one knew anything about pro football. I didn't know if I could make it. Dutch Meyer had offered me a job coaching the freshman team at TCU, and I told [Redskins owner] Mr. [George Preston] Marshall I was going to stay in Texas and coach."[6]

About this time, however, Baugh was selected to play for the College All-Stars, who each year would play a game against the NFL champions. It was this game that helped convince him that he could play at the pro level. "I realized I could play better than ninety-nine percent of them," he remembered. "I became a little more confident about whether or not I could play pro football. As it turned out, we beat Green Bay and then Mr. Marshall got after me pretty hot."[7]

Marshall particularly needed someone who could add some sparkle to pro football. The whole nation was in the throes of hard economic times, and even the relatively modest cost of a ticket was

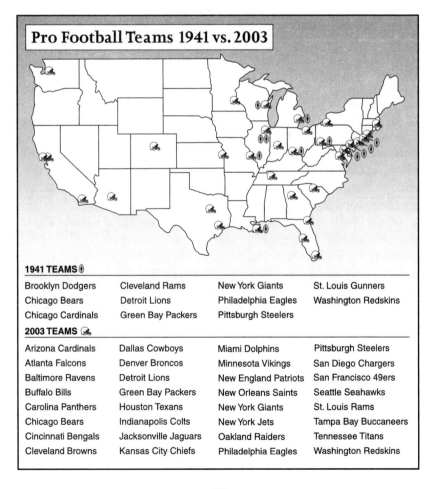

Pro Football Teams 1941 vs. 2003

1941 TEAMS

Brooklyn Dodgers	Cleveland Rams	New York Giants	St. Louis Gunners
Chicago Bears	Detroit Lions	Philadelphia Eagles	Washington Redskins
Chicago Cardinals	Green Bay Packers	Pittsburgh Steelers	

2003 TEAMS

Arizona Cardinals	Dallas Cowboys	Miami Dolphins	Pittsburgh Steelers
Atlanta Falcons	Denver Broncos	Minnesota Vikings	San Diego Chargers
Baltimore Ravens	Detroit Lions	New England Patriots	San Francisco 49ers
Buffalo Bills	Green Bay Packers	New Orleans Saints	Seattle Seahawks
Carolina Panthers	Houston Texans	New York Giants	St. Louis Rams
Chicago Bears	Indianapolis Colts	New York Jets	Tampa Bay Buccaneers
Cincinnati Bengals	Jacksonville Jaguars	Oakland Raiders	Tennessee Titans
Cleveland Browns	Kansas City Chiefs	Philadelphia Eagles	Washington Redskins

a luxury for many fans. Like other NFL teams, the Redskins—who were Eastern Division champions in 1936—were having trouble drawing fans. With attendance down, the team relocated to Washington prior to the 1937 season. Desperate for a star to attract customers, Marshall signed Baugh to a contract calling for a yearly salary of eight thousand dollars, making him the highest-paid player on the team. In an effort to generate publicity, Marshall also tried to foster an image of Baugh as a Texas cowboy, despite the fact that he was a city boy. Marshall gave him a five-hundred-dollar bonus and told him to dress in a cowboy outfit for his contract-signing ceremony. Baugh complied and, wearing high-heeled cowboy boots and a ten-gallon hat, Baugh was introduced to Washington fans.

A Title for the Rookie

Baugh may have been an imitation cowboy, but on the field he proved that the stories about his passing ability were true. According to legend, at the team's first practice, Washington coach Ray Flaherty tossed Baugh a football. "Let's see you hit that receiver in the eye," he said, looking toward end Wayne Millner. "Which eye?"[8] asked the confident Baugh.

Baugh backed up his words with his play in games. He started the year at tailback on offense (and also as defensive back). In his very first game, he completed eleven of sixteen passes for 116 yards to lead the Redskins to victory over the New York Giants. He continued his solid play all year long, guiding Washington to a first-place finish in the Eastern Division while completing a league-record eighty-one passes.

In the NFL Championship Game against the Chicago Bears, Baugh was even more spectacular. With Washington trailing 14-7 at halftime, he led them back by completing touchdown tosses of 55, 78, and 35 yards in the third quarter. The rookie threw for a championship-game-record 354 yards, completing a memorable first season by helping the Redskins win the first title in their history by a score of 28-21.

Revolutionizing the Pro Game

With Baugh leading the Washington attack, the Redskins were perennial contenders for the NFL title. In his first nine seasons, he guided the team to five league championship games by making the pass an integral part of the offense. Opponents were often taken by surprise. Until Baugh came along, teams had used the pass mainly as a third-down desperation play. Baugh, on the other hand, would throw on any down and from any part of the field, even deep in the opponent's territory.

In 1940, Baugh surprised opponents with 111 completions, good for a league-leading 1,367 yards and twelve touchdowns. He also led the circuit in punting, averaging 51.4 yards per kick. That mark has yet to be exceeded, and is a record that Baugh is extremely proud of. "I have had more skill than any [person] who ever punted a football," he notes. "They punt the ball high and down the middle of the field nowadays. . . . We punted to corners, to the right or left, and it's something you never see anymore. We'd drop that ball out of bounds on the 6-yard line without letting that [opposing player] touch it."[9]

Still, Baugh and the Redskins had their share of disappointment. For example, in 1940 the Redskins' opponents in the championship game were the mighty Chicago Bears. Washington had defeated Chicago by a score of 7-3 during the regular season. Many Redskins players worried when owner Marshall publicly taunted the Bears after that game, fearing that their vanquished foes would have their revenge should the teams play in the postseason. "He put things in the paper running the Bears down," said Baugh. "You don't want to help the other team [by doing that]."[10]

Baugh's concerns were borne out. The Bears responded by handing the Redskins a 73-0 defeat, the most lopsided score in league history. From the beginning of the game, it seemed that nothing would go right for the Redskins. Following Chicago's first touchdown, Baugh threw a pass that a teammate dropped in the end zone. After the game, a reporter asked him if the outcome of the game would have been different if the pass had been caught. "Yeah," replied Baugh. "I suppose it would have made it 73-7."[11]

The Redskins gained a measure of revenge two years later. The Bears dominated the NFL in 1942, compiling an 11-0 record and outscoring opponents 376 to 84. When they met the Redskins for the championship, Washington came out on top, 14-6, as Baugh tossed a 38-yard touchdown pass to Wilbur Moore, intercepted a Sid Luckman pass, and kept the Bears pinned deep in their own territory by punting for a 52.5-yard average into a strong wind. "Baugh was a headache with the unexpected," said legendary Bears coach George Halas. "It is a principle that you should never kick against a strong wind if it can be avoided, yet Baugh quick-kicked several times on third down with the wind almost dead in his face. He tackled that wind like a sailor. That game was my disappointment of a lifetime."[12]

Following the season, Baugh returned to the ranch he had bought in Rotan, Texas, the year before. He lived there with his

Sammy Baugh's Washington Redskins take on the Chicago Bears in a 1942 game. Baugh led the Redskins to five league championship games.

wife, Edmonia, whom he had married in 1938. They would eventually raise their five children there. Baugh loved the wide-open spaces of his home state and was anxious to return to the more relaxed lifestyle the ranch offered him. In future years, his wife would meet him in the players' parking lot outside of Washington's Griffith Stadium after the final game of the year. She would have the car and kids packed, and the family would head back home to Texas until the following season.

A Magical Season

In 1943, Baugh had what is arguably the greatest year ever by a football player. As a single wing tailback on offense, he led the NFL in pass attempts, pass completions, and completion percentage while throwing for 1,754 yards. On defense, he topped the league in interceptions. He also led the circuit in punting for the fourth consecutive year. In the modern era, such a feat is unheard of since teams emphasize specialization and nobody has the opportunity to dominate in three separate areas.

On November 14, 1943, the skinny Texan intercepted an NFL-record four passes in a game against the Detroit Lions. (He also threw for four touchdowns.) Baugh, however, downplayed the feat in his typically modest fashion, saying:

> I've got two fine cornerbacks to the side of me, Wilbur Moore and Dick Todd. They're as good as anybody playing that day.

> Here I am, the weak one in there. And I know it. They tackle better than I could. They were better defensive men than I was so who do you think those quarterbacks over there are going to work on, me or Wilbur or Dick?[13]

Baugh's magical season ended on a negative note. Once again facing the Bears for the title, he suffered a concussion early in the first quarter while tackling Sid Luckman and was forced to leave the game. The Bears proceeded to take the championship with a 41-21 win.

A New Formation

For 1944, the Redskins' offense switched from the wing formation to the T (in which the fullback and halfbacks lined up behind the quarterback, forming the letter *T*). The formation was much more conducive to a passing attack than the wing. In the wing, the tailback lined up as a blocking back. In the T, the quarterback received the snap directly behind the center.

Despite some initial apprehension, Baugh soon grew to love the new formation. As he said, "The wear and tear on a T quarterback was about half what it was on a tailback."[14] He proceeded to rewrite the record book, leading the NFL in passing in 1945, 1947, and 1949. He recorded highs of 210 complete passes, 2,938 yards passing, and 25 touchdown passes in 1947, and an incredible 70.3 completion percentage in 1945 (still the second-highest mark ever). In the latter year, he led Washington to the title game for the fifth time, but the Redskins were defeated there by the Cleveland Rams, 15-14.

One rainy November day in 1947, Baugh was honored by the Touchdown Club of Washington with Sammy Baugh Day. After the ceremonies (during which he was presented with a new station wagon), Baugh went out to have perhaps his best game as a pro. Playing the powerful Chicago Cardinals, he completed eleven of his first thirteen passes. He finished the game with six touchdown passes and 355 yards thrown while leading Washington to a 45-21 victory.

A New Generation

By the late 1940s, a whole new generation of passing quarterbacks had begun to appear on the scene. Bob Waterfield, Otto Graham, Paul Christman, Charlie Conerly, Frankie Albert, Johnny Lujack, Bobby Layne, and Norm Van Brocklin were part of this new wave of talent. Baugh, however, was still going strong. In 1949, at age thirty-five, he led the NFL in completion percentage for the seventh time with a mark of 56.9 percent.

By that time, however, Baugh realized that his glory days were over. He played three more years with Washington before retiring

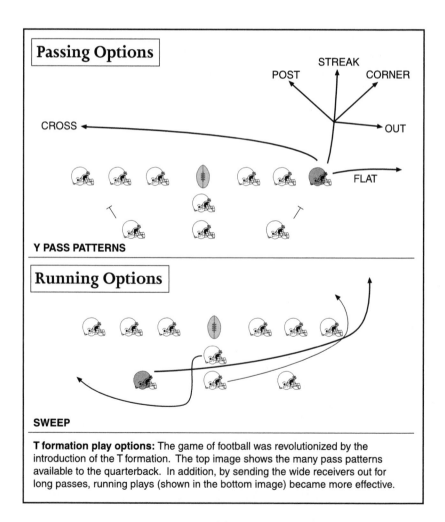

T formation play options: The game of football was revolutionized by the introduction of the T formation. The top image shows the many pass patterns available to the quarterback. In addition, by sending the wide receivers out for long passes, running plays (shown in the bottom image) became more effective.

after the 1952 season. He left Washington and returned home to his beloved Texas. "I was always so damn glad to get out of Washington," he said. "I enjoyed those years, but I always got out of there as fast as I could. I don't like any damn city, and that's all there is to it. I don't enjoy it one bit."[15]

Baugh's love of football eventually drew him back to the game as a coach, but he was far less successful than he had been as a player. In 1955, Baugh was offered the head coaching job at Hardin-Simmons University in Abilene, Texas. He stayed there three years, compiling a 23-28 record. In 1960, the fledgling American Football League came into existence as a challenger to the NFL. Baugh was named as the first head coach of the New York Titans. He compiled a 7-7 record in each of his two years with the team. Three years later, he took over the same position with the league's Houston Oilers, whom he guided to a 4-10 mark in 1964. After stepping down at Houston, he retired to his farm in Rotan.

An NFL Legend

Despite the disappointing experience in coaching, Baugh's place in NFL history is secure. When he entered the league, football was struggling to establish itself on the professional level. By the time he retired, pro football was well on its way to becoming a national phenomenon, thanks in part to the excitement he helped bring to the game. As the *Washington Post* editorial page stated upon Baugh's retirement, "Washington, especially in the autumn months, will be a duller and sadder place."[16]

At the time of his retirement, Baugh was the NFL career leader in every major passing category. Although his records have since been surpassed, he still holds two punting marks. No one has ever beaten his single-season average of 51.4 yards set in 1940, nor his career mark of 45.1 yards per punt. For his accomplishments on the field of play, Baugh was selected by members of the news media as one of the charter members of the Professional Football Hall of Fame in 1963.

Since retiring, Baugh has lived a relatively secluded life on his beloved ranch in Rotan. He was an avid golfer until his knees began to give him problems. As he closes in on his ninetieth birthday, he still follows football closely and watches as many games as he can.

CHAPTER 2

Otto Graham: The Winner

Longtime Dallas Cowboys coach Tom Landry once said:

> When you talk about the greatest quarterbacks, you talk first about the winners. That list necessarily starts with Otto Graham. Ten championship game appearances in ten years . . . makes him the greatest winner in pro football history. . . . To many people, that one thing is the ultimate proof of the quality of a quarterback. It is what the position is all about.[17]

Graham's poise, leadership, and unerring passing accuracy helped make him pro football's ultimate winner.

A Multitalented Youngster

Otto Everett Graham Jr. was born in Waukegan, Illinois, on December 6, 1921, one of four sons born to Otto Sr. and his wife. The elder Grahams were both music teachers and were determined to pass on their love of the arts to their children. As he grew up, young Otto learned to play the piano, violin, cornet, and French horn. He was also interested in sports and became proficient in all that he tried, particularly baseball, basketball, and football. Otto's parents encouraged him in all his pursuits—artistic, academic, and athletic. He was taught the value of an education and was motivated to do his best in everything he tried.

When Otto entered Waukegan High School (where his father was the band director), he showed real promise as a musician. At age sixteen, he became the Illinois French horn state champion and played in the Waukegan National Champion brass sextet. Otto had always been a big kid, and on the athletic field his size helped him gain an edge over his opponents. He was the conference scoring champion in basketball that same year. In 1938, he not only played both basketball and football but was good enough to make the All-State squad in both sports. As a triple-threat tailback (passing, running, and kicking), the highlight of Otto's high school football career came in a game against the state champ, Dundee High School. He scored twenty points for the Waukegan Bulldogs as they upset Dundee, ending that school's three-year, forty-four-game winning streak in the process.

Despite being so involved in sports, Otto was able to keep up with his schoolwork. He graduated early and received numerous athletic scholarship offers. After narrowing his choices down to Northwestern University or Dartmouth College, he eventually accepted a full basketball scholarship to Northwestern, in nearby Evanston, Illinois.

Otto Graham poses with one of his many trophies. Graham originally attended Northwestern University to play basketball, but he soon joined their football team.

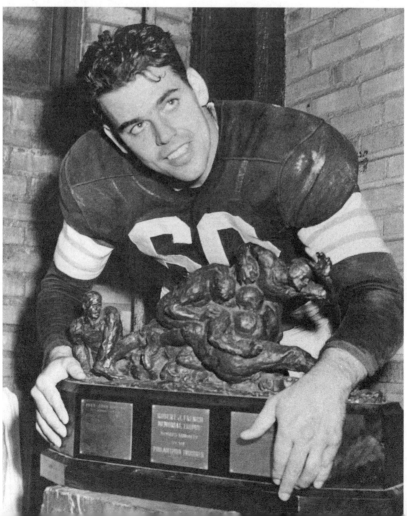

A Wildcat Legend

At Northwestern, Graham majored in music. He was a featured player in the school's orchestra, but it was in athletics that he truly blossomed. He starred on the basketball team and made second-team All-America his junior season. The next year, he was named captain of the Wildcats squad. He was the second-leading scorer in the Big Ten Conference and his team's most valuable player. Graham topped off his year by being named first-team All-America. The versatile Graham also played baseball for the Wildcats and was the team's third-leading batter.

It was in football, however, that Graham earned his greatest acclaim, even though he had not been invited to try out for the football team as a freshman. He was playing intramural football that year when he caught the eye of Lynn "Pappy" Waldorf, coach of the varsity squad. Waldorf was impressed by the strong-armed freshman and convinced him to come out for spring practice. Once there, Graham stole the show. He ran for three touchdowns and threw for three more in the annual spring scrimmage, cementing his spot on the team.

Graham was the Wildcats' starting tailback from his sophomore season of 1941 through 1943. He smashed many Big Ten passing records along the way, throwing for a total of 2,072 yards in his career and 1,092 in his junior season. He set one Northwestern record by returning a punt ninety-three yards and another by scoring twenty-seven points in a game against Wisconsin. Of the latter contest, Walter Paulison wrote in his book *The Tale of the Wildcats:* "Graham had a field day at Madison in the course of a 41 to 0 brush with Wisconsin. Otto contributed three touchdowns and three extra points in the first 12 minutes, returned a punt 45 yards for a touchdown in the third period, and tossed a fifth score to Wallis."[18]

In the final game of his collegiate career, Graham led the Wildcats to a 53-6 trouncing of Illinois. Wrote Paulison: "And for an appropriate conclusion to his career he ran onto the field at game's end, clad in civilian clothes, grabbed the ball over which the teams were fighting, and ran off with it. He also ran off with the *Chicago Tribune* silver football award as the most valuable player in the Conference."[19]

Yet perhaps the most pivotal game in Graham's football career had come in 1941, when he led Northwestern to a 14-7 upset victory over the powerful Ohio State team. Paul Brown, coach of the Buckeyes, was duly impressed with the young sophomore. In later years, he would have a profound influence on Graham's career.

Playing for Northwestern, Otto Graham runs for a first down against Michigan. After college, Graham joined the U.S. Navy Air Corps, where he improved his game.

Paul Brown and the Browns

At the time Graham was finishing out his college career, the United States was deeply involved in World War II, and able-bodied young men were either volunteering or being drafted for military service. Graham took a commission as an officer in the U.S. Navy Air Corps. After preflight training, Graham was transferred to a training facility in Chapel Hill, North Carolina. There he became cadet regimental commander. It was there, too, that he played football on a team consisting of other former college players coached by Paul "Bear" Bryant. Under Bryant, Graham learned the intricacies of a new formation, the T, in which the quarterback stood directly behind the center.

While serving out his enlistment, Graham was approached by Brown, who was forming a team to play in the new All-America Football Conference (AAFC), which team owners hoped would one day compete with the NFL. The team, named for their coach, was the Cleveland Browns. Having remembered Graham from watching him play at Northwestern, Brown thought he would be a perfect T formation quarterback. "Poise, ballhandling and leadership," said Brown. "Otto has the basic requirements of a T quarterback."[20]

Brown wanted to make sure he did not lose Graham's services to another team, so he made him an offer he could not refuse. Recalled Graham: "I was getting a naval cadet's pay in World War II when Brown came out to the station and offered me a two-year contract at $7,500 per. He also offered me a $1,000 bonus and $250 a month for the duration of the war. All I asked was, 'Where do I sign?' Old Navy men say I rooted for the war to last forever."[21]

Upon the war's end, Graham returned to civilian life. Before reporting to the Browns, however, he signed a contract to play basketball with the Rochester Royals. The six-foot-five-inch, 205-pound Graham was a substitute guard on the 1946 team that won the National Basketball League championship. Graham played just one season of professional basketball, then joined the Browns.

The All-America Football Conference

By scouting and signing players who had been in the service, Brown had put together a solid core from which to build his team. When the AAFC began playing in 1946, the Cleveland Browns

Playing for the Cleveland Browns, Graham makes a pass. Before joining the Browns, Graham played one season of professional basketball.

were clearly the most powerful team in the league. They compiled a 12-2 record that first year, then met New York's AAFC team, the Yankees, for the league championship.

In the title contest, Graham led Cleveland to a 14-9 come-from-behind victory. He completed sixteen of twenty-seven passes for 213 yards, with the winning score coming on a 16-yard scoring toss to Dante Lavelli with just five minutes remaining. The Yankees threatened to come back, but their late rally was snuffed out when Graham, playing on defense, intercepted a New York pass. By leading the Browns to the title, Graham became the first pro athlete to play on two championship teams in different sports in the same year. In appreciation of his performance, Brown tore up Graham's original two-year contract and increased his salary to twelve thousand dollars a year.

The Browns repeated their success over the next three years, dominating the league during the regular season and winning the championship each year. Graham proved himself the ultimate team player in that he let his coach decide the plays—something other quarterbacks at that time would have resisted. Brown sent the plays in from the bench, and Graham executed them precisely, just as he had in college when he earned the nickname "Automatic Otto." "I never openly criticized the coach," he said. "We had a checkoff system [one in which the quarterback can change a play at the line of scrimmage by calling an audible], and occasionally I'd change one of his plays, but as for his calling the game, we never talked about it. He was the admiral, the general, the CEO."[22]

Besides having plays called from the sidelines, what set the Browns apart was their reliance on the pass to move the ball. Graham explained:

> We were a passing team in the era of the run. But we could still dominate with the run, too. . . . My talents? I could throw hard if I had to, I could lay it up soft, I could drill the sideline pass. . . . We developed the timed sideline pass, the comeback route where the receiver goes to the sideline, stops, and comes back to the ball. Everything thrown on rhythm.[23]

On to the National Football League

Thanks in large measure to the smooth relationship between Graham and his coach, the Browns dominated play in the AAFC. Still, most observers did not believe they could ever play as well as the teams of the NFL. Graham got his chance to prove them wrong when the AAFC folded following the 1949 season and the two leagues agreed that three of the defunct league's teams, the Browns, the San Francisco 49ers, and the Baltimore Colts, would join the NFL.

Graham and his teammates believed they were every bit as good as NFL players. The NFL's commissioner, Bert Bell, believed otherwise. In an attempt to teach the confident newcomers a lesson, Bell arranged the 1950 schedule so that Cleveland's first game was against the NFL-champion Philadelphia Eagles.

Graham's first NFL pass proved his confidence was well-founded: It was good for a touchdown, and Cleveland proceeded to stun Philadelphia by winning by a score of 35-10. A crowd of 71,237 looked on as Graham threw for three touchdown passes and a total of 346 yards through the air. The humiliated coach of the Eagles tried to disparage the Browns' performance by suggesting that they were not playing real football. "After the game against the Eagles, their coach, Greasy Neale, said we were nothing but a basketball team. Pretty good basketball team, huh?"[24]

Graham and the Browns proved the contest had not been a fluke. Cleveland finished its inaugural NFL season with a record of 10 and 2. Graham completed 137 of 253 pass attempts for 1,943 yards and fourteen touchdowns, and he was named the league's player of the year.

In the championship game, the Browns were matched up against the Los Angeles Rams. Graham directed Cleveland to four touchdowns, but his team trailed by a point with just minutes to go. With time running out, he led the Browns downfield into Rams territory. There, kicker Lou Groza connected on a sixteen-yard field goal with twenty seconds left to give Cleveland a 30-28 victory and the championship. Incredibly, Graham had now led his team to five titles in five years of play.

The Road Back to the Top

Over the next three seasons, the Browns won more games than any other NFL club. In the process, Graham solidified his status as the league's premiere quarterback. He twice led the circuit in yards passing while topping the charts in passes attempted, passes completed, and touchdown passes one time each. In 1953, his performance earned him player of the year honors for the second time.

One game that season gave testimony to Graham's toughness as a player. While playing the San Francisco 49ers on November 15, he was knocked out of bounds and elbowed in the face by linebacker Art Michalik in the first half. Graham was taken out of the game and received thirteen stitches to close the cut in the corner of his mouth. He was determined to get back in, however, so a clear plastic bar was attached to the front of his helmet. "That's my real claim to fame right there," said Graham. "I was the first guy who ever wore a face mask—college, high school or pro."[25] Graham returned to action determined to make the 49ers pay. With 80,698 fans cheering his every move, Graham came back to lead the Browns to a 23-21 win.

Despite Graham's heroics during the regular season, Cleveland lost the NFL Championship Game each of those three years—to the Rams in 1951 (24-17) and to the Detroit Lions in 1952 (17-7) and 1953 (17-16). The 1953 contest was Graham's worst game as a professional. He completed just two of fifteen passes, yet kept the Browns in the game until the very end.

At age thirty-three, Graham bounced back the next year to lead the Browns to yet another Eastern Conference crown. Throwing fewer passes than in previous seasons, he led the NFL in passing percentage for the second year in a row.

In the championship contest against Detroit, Graham was a one-man wrecking crew. He threw three touchdown passes of 35, 8, and 31 yards, and completed nine of twelve passes for 163 yards. In addition, he scored three times himself in leading the Browns to a 56-10 rout of the Lions. The win was Graham's sixth championship in nine pro seasons.

One Last Hurrah

Following the game, Graham announced his retirement as a player. He cited mental pressures and time spent away from his family as his reasons for leaving. To coach Paul Brown, however, he intimated that he would return if Brown could not find an adequate replacement for him.

Graham's backup, George Ratterman, was set to take over the starting job, but a poor preseason caused Brown to rethink that plan. He convinced Graham to come back for one more year by offering him a contract for twenty-five thousand dollars, making him the highest-paid player in the league. Returning in time for the last exhibition game, Graham won back his starting job and did not miss a beat. In his tenth season at quarterback, he led the league in completion percentage while guiding his club to a 9-2-1 record.

Graham ended his pro career as he had started it, leading Cleveland to a 38-14 win over the Rams in the NFL Championship Game.

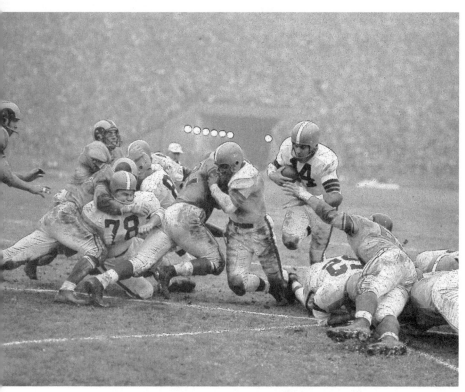

Graham drives past the Los Angeles Rams defense to score the final touchdown of his career in the 1955 NFL Championship Game.

He threw for 209 yards and a pair of touchdowns and ran for two scores himself. As Graham walked off the field at the Los Angeles Memorial Coliseum for the last time, he was greeted with a standing ovation from the 85,693 fans in attendance. As a touched Graham fondly recalled in the NFL Films documentary, *The Cleveland Browns—Fifty Years of Memories*, "You don't find that happening too often in professional sports, where the opposition—the fans—who hate your guts, to put it mildly, will stand up and give you a standing ovation."[26]

A Second Career

Graham's playing days had ended, but he remained committed to football and turned his attention to coaching. He began in 1958 by guiding the College All-Stars in their annual game against the defending NFL champions. He led the college squad to victory twice, against the Lions in 1958 and the Green Bay Packers in 1963. (In the forty-two games played in the series, the collegiates won only seven other times.)

In 1959, Graham accepted the position of athletic director and head football coach at the U.S. Coast Guard Academy. He remained there until taking over at the helm of the Washington Redskins in 1966. In Washington, his passing-oriented squad, led by quarterback Sonny Jurgensen, compiled a 17-22-3 record in three seasons. Graham was replaced by Vince Lombardi in 1969 and returned to the Coast Guard Academy as athletic director. He remained there for sixteen more years until retiring in 1985. Since then, he has lived in Sarasota, Florida. Showing the same determination as he did on the football field, he defeated colorectal cancer in 1978. Unfortunately, he is currently in the early stages of Alzheimer's disease, for which there is no known cure.

In addition to ten championship games and seven titles in ten incredible seasons, Graham's career passing record shows a completion rate of 55.8 percent, 174 touchdowns, and 23,584 total yards. His 9.0 yards per passing attempt is the highest mark of any quarterback with one thousand or more throws. Graham led the league in passing yardage on six occasions and was named most valuable player six times.

Graham was elected to the Professional Football Hall of Fame in 1965 in his first year of eligibility. He was named to the NFL's 75th Anniversary Team in 1994 and as one of the one hundred top athletes of the millennium by ESPN five years later. Despite all his awards and statistics, his legacy was simply stated by Paul Brown. "The test of a quarterback is where his team finishes," said his former coach. "By that standard, Otto was the best of them all."[27]

CHAPTER 3

Johnny Unitas: The Battler

Johnny Unitas was a master craftsperson on the football field. Although he did not possess outstanding physical tools, no quarterback was better at picking apart opposing defenses. Unitas was also fearless, confident, and cool under pressure. His fierce determination and refusal to give up helped him make it to the NFL in

Baltimore Colts quarterback legend Johnny Unitas throws a touchdown pass in a 1972 game. Unitas is credited, in part, for increasing the popularity of pro football.

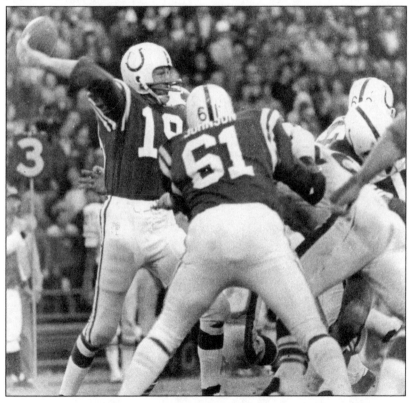

the first place. To those who follow football, another of Unitas's claims to fame is the 1958 NFL Championship Game, in which he led his Baltimore Colts team to an overtime victory over the New York Giants, in the process sparking the growth in popularity of pro football.

From the Foothills of Pennsylvania

John Constantine Unitas was born in Pittsburgh on May 7, 1933. His father, Leonard, was a Lithuanian immigrant who owned a truck and ran a coal delivery service. Leonard Unitas, however, was not destined to be a part of his son's life: When Johnny was five years old, Leonard contracted pneumonia and died. Johnny's mother, Helen, took over the business and also worked nights in order to support her four children—Johnny, his older brother, Len, and his sisters, Millicent and Shirley. Helen eventually went to night school and became a bookkeeper for the city of Pittsburgh.

Somehow, Helen managed to provide for the family of five. When Johnny got older, he helped out by getting odd jobs to bring in money. In addition to keeping him physically fit, the jobs helped him learn responsibility. With his mother as a role model, Johnny developed a work ethic that would serve him well in future years.

As a youngster, Johnny had several near brushes with disaster. When he was five, he had fallen out of his father's truck and was nearly run over. Two years later, an even more serious accident befell Johnny. He and his brother were throwing rocks at a bullet cartridge they found. As he remembered, "It exploded . . . and I was standing right in front of it and got most of the stuff in my leg."[28]

Despite these accidents Johnny thrived and became a star athlete at St. Justin's High School in Pittsburgh. When he tried out for the football team as a sophomore, the coach used him at halfback and end. Shortly before the team's first game of the season, however, the quarterback broke his ankle. Johnny started and was the quarterback from that point on.

As a senior in 1950, Unitas was named to the Pittsburgh All-Catholic High School team. He received glowing notices in the local papers, including one from Wilbert Rall, the coach at the competing St. Wendelin's High School. "Unitas has been a real workhorse for his team and his coach," said Rall. "He was the backbone of the St. Justin's ball club with his field generalship, his passing, kicking, running and defensive play. He's a very quiet and unassuming boy, but he's a package of dynamite on a football field. He's by far one of the finest passers in scholastic football."[29]

By this time, Unitas had his heart set on becoming a professional football player. He hoped to get a scholarship to play ball in college and dreamed of playing for the University of Notre Dame. Unfortunately, the Notre Dame coaches thought Unitas was too skinny to play quarterback. At six feet tall and 138 pounds, they did not think he would be able to take the constant pounding he would receive. Indiana University also turned him down for the same reason. Unitas finally received a scholarship offer from the University of Louisville. He accepted it and began there in the fall of 1951, determined to prove he could be a success at that level.

Disappointment

Unitas started his freshman year as third-string quarterback. The team got off to a slow start and lost its first three games. His coach decided he might as well give the freshman some experience and started him in the fourth game. Unitas nearly led the team to victory as they lost by a single point to St. Bonaventure. By the fifth game of the season, Unitas had taken over the starting job while also playing safety on defense.

Louisville had a 5-4 record that year, but graduation losses hit the school hard. Over the next three seasons, they would win a total of just seven games while losing nineteen. Unitas considered transferring to Indiana but decided against it. He compiled solid statistics in his four years, completing 48.5 percent of his passes for 2,984 yards and twenty-seven touchdowns. His best game came against Florida State University in his sophomore year. That day, Unitas completed seventeen of twenty-two passes with three touchdowns in a 41-14 Louisville victory.

When the NFL held its annual draft in 1954, the Pittsburgh Steelers made Unitas their ninth pick. Unitas, though, never received much of a chance with Pittsburgh. Coach Walt Kiesling told him he had more quarterbacks than he could use, and Unitas did not play in any of the team's five exhibition games. Unitas was finally cut from the squad and returned home to take a job with a construction gang.

Yet Unitas held on to his dream of playing football for a living. While working in construction, Unitas signed on to play with the Bloomfield Rams, a semipro team in the Greater Pittsburgh League. "They called it semipro football," he recalled. "Actually it was just sandlot, a bunch of guys knocking the hell out of each other on an oil-soaked field under the Bloomfield Bridge."[30] Unitas received six dollars a game, but the money mattered little. "What I needed," he said, "was a chance to prove that I could play football."[31] He got that chance in February 1956 when he received a call from Don Kellett, the general manager of the Baltimore Colts.

A Second Chance

Kellett offered Unitas the opportunity to work out for Colts coach Weeb Ewbank in April. Ewbank liked what he saw of the youngster. The Colts signed Unitas to a contract calling for the league minimum of seven thousand dollars. As Ewbank explained, "Unitas

Johnny Unitas was recruited to play for the Baltimore Colts in 1956. His debut with the team was less than spectacular, but in games that followed he demonstrated his full potential.

was signed after we received a letter from a fan telling us there was a player in Bloomington deserving a chance. I always accused Johnny of writing it."[32]

With veteran George Shaw at quarterback, the Colts got off to a 1-2 start in 1956. In the fourth game of the year against the Chicago Bears, Shaw was injured, and Unitas came in to replace him. His debut was less than glorious as he threw an interception on his first pass. The Bears won by a score of 58-27, and Unitas was downcast as he sat in the locker room after the game. Baltimore owner Carroll Rosenbloom came over to him and said, "Now look, John, that was not your fault. You haven't had an opportunity to play and no one is blaming you. You're not only going to be a good one in this league, you are going to be a *great* one."[33]

Unitas bounced back to lead the Colts to a 28-21 win over the Green Bay Packers the following week. Baltimore defeated the Cleveland Browns in their next game, and Unitas's hold on the quarterback's job was cemented.

On December 9, Unitas completed a touchdown pass for the Colts' only score in a 31-7 loss to the Los Angeles Rams. Despite the loss, that game marked the beginning of an incredible streak for Unitas. Over the next four years, he would throw touchdown passes in forty-seven consecutive games, an NFL record which has yet to be broken.

In his first season, Unitas completed 55.6 percent of his throws (a higher percentage than any rookie before him) for 1,498 yards and nine touchdowns as the Colts finished in fourth place in the Western Conference of the NFL with a record of 5-7. The team improved to 7-5 the next season as he led the league in pass attempts (301), passing yardage (2,550), and touchdown passes (24). The stage was set for him to burst into national prominence in 1958.

The Greatest Game Ever Played

With Unitas at the helm, the Colts got off to a fast start in 1958, defeating the Lions, Bears, and Packers in their first three contests. In the third game, however, Unitas was kneed in the middle of his back and was sidelined with three broken ribs and a punctured lung. Although the next day's papers said he was through for the year, he surprised everyone by returning to action three weeks later, wearing a special corset. On Baltimore's first play from scrimmage that day, Unitas connected with his halfback Lenny Moore for a fifty-eight yard touchdown pass.

Unitas runs the ball in the 1958 NFL Championship Game against the New York Giants, a game many fans still consider the greatest game ever played.

Despite missing two games that year, Unitas again led the league in touchdown passes. He was starting to gain recognition as the best quarterback in the league for his ability to work under pressure, his accuracy as a passer, and his toughness. That toughness became his signature trait. Said Los Angeles Rams defensive tackle Merlin Olsen, "I often thought that sometimes he'd hold the ball one count longer than he had to just so he could take the hit and laugh in your face."[34]

The Colts finished the year at 9-3 to top the Western Conference. On December 28, 1958, they faced off against the New York Giants for the title. With 64,185 fans packing New York's Yankee Stadium and over 50 million more watching on television, the two teams met in what many people still consider the greatest game ever played in the history of the NFL.

Throughout the game, the lead shifted back and forth. With less than two minutes to go, the Colts found themselves trailing by three points. Unitas led his offense out on the field, determined to bring his club back. With time running out and the pressure squarely on his shoulders, he threw an eleven-yard pass to Lenny Moore for a first down. Following an incompletion, he then threw three consecutive passes to Raymond Berry to bring the Colts to

New York's thirteen-yard line. "Once the Colts got the ball," remembered public address announcer Bob Sheppard, "it seemed like I was stuttering, 'Unitas to Berry, Unitas to Berry, Unitas to Berry, Unitas to Berry.' I wanted to shout into my microphone, 'Will someone cover Berry?'"[35] Steve Myhra's twenty-yard field goal with seven seconds left tied the game and sent it into overtime, the first in NFL Championship Game history.

The Giants received the kickoff to start overtime. They fell short of making a first down by a foot, and were forced to punt. Baltimore took over on its own twenty-yard line, and the unflappable Unitas proceeded to move them down the field. Mixing sweeps, draw plays, and passes to Berry, he got them to the one-yard line. There, fullback Alan Ameche rumbled into the end zone for the game-winning score. The Colts had their first world championship.

Unitas was named the game's most valuable player. Giants linebacker Sam Huff put Unitas's performance in perspective. "A lot of people look back," said Huff, "and say if we'd covered Ray Berry better that day, we'd have won. Not true. It was Unitas. If we'd stopped Berry, Unitas would've done the same thing with Lenny Moore. Unitas was great that day."[36]

Despite what some say about the legacy of his outstanding performance, Unitas refused to take credit for helping to bring football into the national spotlight. "I've always felt that it wasn't a real good football game until the last two minutes, and then the overtime," he said. "Just the fact that it was the first overtime in championship play, and it happened in Madison Avenue's [the advertising industry's] backyard, that was enough to make people feel they had seen something fantastic."[37]

The Legend Grows

Unitas led the Colts to another championship in 1959. He set new career highs for pass attempts, pass completions, passing yardage, and touchdown passes (with an NFL record of thirty-two), leading the league in all four categories. He was named the NFL's most valuable player for the first of three times.

In the championship game, the Colts again defeated the Giants. After Baltimore scored first on a sixty-yard pass from Unitas to Moore, the Giants came back with three field goals and took a 9-7 lead. Unitas brought the Colts back in the final quarter, scoring once on a four-yard run and tossing another touchdown pass, this time to end Jerry Richardson. Baltimore tallied twenty-four points in the last period to earn a 31-16 victory. Unitas was named the game's most valuable player for the second consecutive year.

The Colts fell to fourth place in the Western Conference in 1960, but through no fault of Unitas's. He again led the league in pass attempts, completions, and passing yardage. His twenty-five touchdown passes topped the NFL for the fourth consecutive season, something no passer had ever done before.

The Colts compiled a mediocre record in the early 1960s, but Unitas continued to shine. For example, he led the league in completions and passing yardage (a career-high 3,481 yards) in 1963, even though his team finished with an 8-6 record. The next year, he guided Baltimore back to a league-best 12-2 record. The Colts lost to the Cleveland Browns in the NFL Championship Game, but Unitas won his second most valuable player award for his performance during the season.

Unitas won his third and final most valuable player award in 1967. That year, he led the NFL with a 58.5 percent completion rate while passing for 3,428 yards and twenty touchdowns. The Colts compiled an 11-1-2 record, but were edged out for the new Coastal Division title by the Rams.

The following year, Unitas tore ligaments in his right elbow and was sidelined for most of the season. At thirty-five years of age, he was finally beginning to show signs of years of wear and tear on

Unitas throws a pass in a 1962 game. Unitas led the Colts to numerous victories and was named most valuable player three times.

his body. The Colts turned to backup quarterback Earl Morrall, who had a career year and led them all the way to Super Bowl III. There, they were eighteen-point favorites over the New York Jets.

Led by brash young quarterback Joe Namath, the underdog New Yorkers dominated the Colts and led 16-0 in the fourth quarter. Unitas came into the game and guided Baltimore on its only scoring drive to close the margin to 16-7. An onside kick gave the Colts the ball back with three minutes left, but New York's defense prevailed. Unitas completed eleven of twenty-four passes in his Super Bowl baptism, but the Jets came away with the title.

Super Bowl V

Unitas bounced back from his injury to put together two more solid seasons. In 1970, he helped the Colts to the Super Bowl once again after guiding the team to an 11-2-1 mark and the top spot in the Eastern Division of the newly formed American Football

Johnny Unitas (left) jokes with a former teammate in 1997. Unitas was inducted into the Professional Football Hall of Fame in 1979.

Conference (AFC). He continued to be successful with a quiet determination that let everyone know who was in charge. As former teammate John Mackey once said of playing with Unitas, "It's like being in a huddle with God."[38]

During Super Bowl V, the Dallas Cowboys jumped out to an early 6-0 lead on a pair of field goals. In the second quarter, Unitas connected with Mackey on a seventy-five-yard-pass play that went for a touchdown to tie the game at 6-6 (the extra point attempt was blocked).

An injury, however, robbed Unitas of the chance to lead Baltimore to a Super Bowl victory. Later in the half, he was tackled by Dallas defensive end George Andrie while attempting to pass. He suffered bruised ribs and hobbled to the sidelines. Unitas was replaced by Morrall, who brought the Colts back and led them to a 16-13 victory.

The End of the Line

An off-season torn Achilles tendon suffered while playing paddleball could not keep Unitas from coming back in 1971. He led the Colts to a 10-4 record and a wild-card berth in the postseason playoffs. Baltimore defeated Cleveland in the AFC divisional contest, but lost to the Miami Dolphins for the conference championship.

At the age of thirty-nine, Unitas's best days were behind him. He played in eight games for the Colts in 1972, the last coming against the Buffalo Bills on December 3. He was benched the remainder of the year and was sold to the San Diego Chargers the following January. Unitas appeared in five games as a backup quarterback for the Chargers in 1973 before deciding to retire. He made the announcement without any fanfare or display. "I came into the league without any fuss," he said. "I'd just as soon leave it that way. There's no difference that I can see in retiring from pro football or quitting a job at the Pennsy Railroad. I did something I wanted to do and went as far as I could go."[39]

At the time of his retirement, Unitas held the NFL career records for pass attempts (5,186), completions (2,830), passing yards (40,239), and touchdown passes (290). He had twenty-six games of three hundred or more yards passing and surpassed the three-thousand-yard mark in a season three times. In addition to his three player of the year awards, he was a five-time All-NFL pick and a ten-time All-Pro selection. Other awards included being named Player of the Decade for the 1960s and being selected as one of four quarterbacks on the NFL's 75th Anniversary Team. In 1979, he receive his sport's highest accolade when he was inducted into the Professional Football Hall of Fame.

Unitas became a business person following his retirement, with interests in restaurants, bowling alleys, and real estate. He was also vice president of sales for a computer electronics firm and chairman of Unitas Management Corporation, a sports management firm. In 1974, he was hired as a football commentator for CBS and remained at the job for five years. Unitas also awarded scholarships through the Johnny Unitas Golden Arm Educational Foundation.

Physical problems continued to follow Unitas. He had both knees replaced and needed coronary bypass surgery following a heart attack in 1993. Nine years later, on September 11, 2002, he suffered another attack while working out at a physical therapy center in Baltimore and died. He was sixty-nine.

Unitas was a master craftsperson who fought against adversity to become one of the greatest quarterbacks of all time. He carried himself with class and performed his job to the best of his ability. What he lacked in arm strength and speed he more than made up for with intelligence, coolness under fire, and a toughness that became legendary. That toughness is perhaps best exemplified by something that happened in a game against the Chicago Bears in 1965. As Vic Carucci, national editor of *NFL Insider* related:

> After being hit hard in the face on a blitz, he went down in a heap, but then pulled himself up from the ground. Blood was gushing from his nose, yet he waved off the Colts' trainer and refused to leave the field. What he did next is almost beyond comprehension: He grabbed a handful of mud from the field, jammed it up his nose to stop the bleeding, and, on the very next play, he dropped back again and threw a touchdown pass to John Mackey. It was as if he were saying, "If you guys think you're going to knock me out of this game or keep me from throwing the ball, you're crazy."[40]

That was Johnny Unitas.

CHAPTER 4

Fran Tarkenton:
The Scrambler

As pro football's first quarterback to gain fame as a scrambler, Fran Tarkenton revolutionized the way the position was played. His daring, improvisational style was exceptional when he joined the Minnesota Vikings. Although the Vikings never won a championship under Tarkenton's leadership, they made it to the Super Bowl three times. By the time he retired, Tarkenton's name was at the top of nearly every major passing chart, due largely to the way he managed to elude opposing tacklers as they closed in on him. Fred Dryer of the Rams once said, "Tackling Tarkenton is like trying to pick up a watermelon seed."[41]

The Minister's Son

Francis Asbury Tarkenton was the youngest of three sons born to the Reverend Dallas Tarkenton Sr. and his wife, Frances. He was born in Richmond, Virginia, on February 3, 1940, and named after Francis Asbury, a missionary who was instrumental in founding the Methodist Episcopal church in the United States in the late eighteenth century.

Fran's father was a preacher in the Pentecostal church. The reverend's life was devoted to his family and his faith. He did not have a strong interest in sports, but he did not discourage his sons from participating in them.

When Fran was five years old, the reverend moved his family to Washington, D.C. It was there that the youngster first became involved in football, playing touch football games in the alleys with his friends. His quickness and ability to evade defenders were a benefit to him there. "We played touch football every day," he later recalled, "and you had to be elusive because the alleys were narrow and you didn't have much room to dodge."[42]

Even at a young age, Fran was an intense competitor with a fierce temper. He eventually learned to control his emotions. His

Minnesota Vikings quarterback Fran Tarkenton readies to make a pass. Tarkenton was a star quarterback in high school who went on to play for the University of Georgia before turning pro.

ability to remain calm under pressure proved to be an asset in his future career.

At age ten, Fran played end on the Merrick Boys Club football team. He dreamed of playing quarterback, however, like his hero, Sammy Baugh of the Washington Redskins. He would soon get his chance.

An Athens Legend

The next year, Fran's father moved the family to Athens, Georgia, where he pursued his doctorate degree at the University of Georgia. Fran soon enrolled at Athens High School, where he was an all-around star. By this time, he already knew he was going to be a professional athlete someday.

Fran was a star quarterback for the Trojans, learning the fundamentals of the game from coach Weyman Sellars. He led the team to the state championship in his junior year of 1955, despite suffering a separated shoulder. Athens defeated Valdosta High School by a score of 41-20 in the championship contest, with Tarkenton scoring a touchdown on a ninety-nine-yard kickoff return.

By the time he graduated, he was one of the most sought-after athletes in the state. He received scholarship offers from several universities around the country, but finally decided to stay home in Athens at the University of Georgia. Tarkenton entered Georgia in the fall of 1957. He proceeded to lead the freshman team to an undefeated season. For doing so, he was named to the All-Southeastern Conference freshman team.

Beginning his sophomore season as the third-string quarterback on the varsity team, Tarkenton soon proved just how intense his competitive spirit could be. The plan was for Tarkenton to practice with the team but only to watch games from the sidelines—a means of giving promising players plenty of coaching without using up their eligibility, which was limited to four years. This practice, known as "redshirting," was common in college sports. In the opening game of the year against the University of Texas, Georgia trailed, 7-0, going into the last quarter. When the Georgia Bulldogs got the ball at their own five-yard line after a Texas punt, Tarkenton ran onto the field before coach Wally Butts had a chance to stop him. "I had been pestering coach Butts to let me go in because that was my personality," remembered Tarkenton. "They wanted to redshirt me and I didn't want to because I thought I could help the team. So I just bolted onto the field. I put myself in."[43] He led the Bulldogs on a ninety-five-yard drive that resulted in a touchdown. A two-point conversion gave Georgia an 8-7 lead. Upset at Tarkenton's rashness, which destroyed his plans to keep the youngster on the team an extra year, Butts kept him out the remainder of the game, which Texas went on to win.

Butt's redshirting of Tarkenton was now lost, but over the next three weeks, the coach played Tarkenton only sporadically. The lack of playing time upset Tarkenton, as did Butts's use of profanity, something that, as a preacher's son, he was unaccustomed to hearing. Tarkenton made up his mind to leave Georgia and transfer to Florida State University. He was talked out of his decision by Quinton Lumpkin, who had been his coach on the freshman team. Lumpkin convinced Tarkenton that Butts's strong words, which were used when players did not perform as he wanted them to, were not aimed at him personally. Tarkenton returned to the team and began to see more action. For their part, the Bulldogs started winning. Seeing that good things happened when Tarkenton was in the game, Butts began to play him even more. Slowly but surely, his opinion of his young quarterback began to rise.

One of Tarkenton's most memorable games came in his junior year. Georgia was playing Auburn University for the conference championship and losing, 13-7, with time running out. Tarkenton led the Bulldogs downfield to the Auburn thirteen-yard line, but there the drive stalled, and they faced a fourth-and-thirteen situation with thirty seconds remaining on the clock. At this point, Tarkenton showed his ability to improvise. As he explained in his autobiography, *Tarkenton*, "I called a time-out but did not go to the sidelines to visit Coach Butts. We just didn't have any plays programed for fourth and thirteen with thirty seconds to go. . . . I drew up a play in the huddle."[44] The young quarterback's call resulted in the winning touchdown, giving Georgia the crown and sending them to the Orange Bowl, where they beat the University of Missouri, 14-0.

Tarkenton ended his career at Georgia by being named All-America as a senior in 1960 while leading the SEC in both total offense and passing. He also made first-team Academic All-America and was named the outstanding back in the Hula Bowl, where he led the East to a 14-7 victory over the West. By this time, many observers agreed with Butts's assessment of his star: "Tarkenton has no superior," said the coach, "as a field general and ball carrier."[45]

The Minnesota Vikings and Norm Van Brocklin

When the NFL held its annual draft right after Christmas, Tarkenton was selected in the third round by the expansion Minnesota Vikings, who were coached by former NFL quarterback Norm Van Brocklin. Tarkenton signed for a package totaling fifteen thousand dollars despite being offered more by the Boston Patriots of the fledgling AFL. His dream had always been to play in the NFL, and now he would have his chance.

The Vikings took the field against the mighty Chicago Bears for their first regular season game ever on September 17, 1961. Veteran quarterback George Shaw started for Minnesota, but after a shaky start Van Brocklin replaced him with Tarkenton. The six-foot, 190-pound rookie proceeded to have one of the most spec-

Tarkenton poses for a publicity shot. Tarkenton played five seasons with the Minnesota Vikings before joining the New York Giants.

tacular debuts by a quarterback in league history. He completed seventeen of twenty-three passes for 250 yards and four touchdowns. He ran for a fifth touchdown himself as the Vikings upset the Bears by a score of 37-13.

Tarkenton continued to start for the Vikings, although in spite of his efforts the team mostly lost. Interestingly, the team's major weakness allowed Tarkenton to employ his greatest asset. The protection in front of him tended to break down, and Tarkenton would be forced to scramble to avoid being tackled for a loss. By doing this, he often gained yardage on the ground or stalled for time until a receiver was able to get open. But even with Tarkenton's scrambling, the Vikings finished last place in the NFL's Western Conference.

Van Brocklin did not necessarily blame his quarterback for the losses, but neither was he enamored with Tarkenton's tendency to scramble, even if the alternative was being sacked. He believed a quarterback should rely on his passing ability and do little if any running. As he explained, "A quarterback should run only from sheer terror. When he is forced to run, you have taken away his effectiveness and made him play your game. He won't beat you running. He'll beat you throwing the ball. That's what he's paid to do."[46]

The coach eventually admitted that some of Tarkenton's scrambling was born of necessity, but he never came to accept his quarterback's maneuvers as part of the Vikings' overall strategy. "The first couple of years," said Van Brocklin, "Francis had to get out of there or get killed. And he was clever with it. But I think due to his youth and immaturity he got to thinking it was pretty cute. It was appealing and it was successful for a while."[47]

Playing for the New York Giants, Fran Tarkenton dodges a tackle. Tarkenton perfected a scrambling technique to avoid being sacked.

If Van Brocklin disliked Tarkenton's scrambling, so, too, did opposing coaches. As Baltimore's Don Shula explained:

> It used to drive you crazy. Tarkenton would scramble all around the backfield, giving ground and going farther back toward his own goal line. Then, just when you thought your defensive lineman had him, he'd duck away and start going back to the line of scrimmage. He'd wander all over the field, just waiting for a receiver to come open. Then he'd complete the pass.[48]

Still, the Vikings compiled just one winning season in the years 1961 to 1966, and the tension between Van Brocklin and Tarkenton increased. It reached the breaking point when Van Brocklin benched Tarkenton for a 1966 game against the Atlanta Falcons. In February of the next year, Tarkenton sent Minnesota general manager Jim Finks a request for a trade, saying that if a deal was not made he would retire.

On to New York

As it happened, Van Brocklin resigned the next day. Tarkenton, however, did not reconsider his request. The Vikings accommodated him by sending him to the New York Giants in early March, even though his statistics argued in favor of keeping him. Tarkenton's first stint with Minnesota ended with him having completed nearly 54 percent of his passes, 113 of which resulted in touchdowns. His scrambling resulted in an average of 6.5 yards gained on each of his 293 carries with the ball.

The Giants' team Tarkenton joined was exceptionally weak, having won only one game the previous season. With him at the helm, the club improved to 7-7 in 1967. Tarkenton had one of the best seasons of his career, completing 54.1 percent of his passes for 3,088 yards and a career-high twenty-nine passing touchdowns. Tarkenton continued to produce solid offensive numbers over the course of four additional seasons with New York. Some even said that he was the primary reason the Giants were able to field a competitive team week after week. As former Giants center Greg Larson recalled, "In a couple of those years, we wouldn't have won a game without Tarkenton."[49]

By 1971, Tarkenton had played eleven seasons in the NFL and had never played in a championship game, let alone the Super Bowl. With the Giants mired in mediocrity, Tarkenton told New York owner Wellington Mara he wanted to be traded, but only to a contending team. As he explained in his autobiography, "If Mara did trade me to a bottom-drawer team, I said I wouldn't report. That was it for me. I'd had it with losing. I'd rather get out of football than have to put up with all of the aggravation from impatient fans, the flak in the media, all the unpleasantness that goes with it."[50]

The Scrambler Returns

Mara arranged to trade Tarkenton back to the Vikings, and the deal was completed that winter. Tarkenton was ecstatic. The Vikings had been transformed into one of the top clubs in the league. Beginning in 1968, they won four straight Central Division titles. Following a 12-2 season in 1969, they made it all the way to the Super Bowl. Van Brocklin was no longer the coach in Minnesota, having been replaced by Bud Grant in 1967. As Tarkenton said, "I have great respect for Van Brocklin as a coach, but not as my coach. I just have too many different ideas about football."[51]

Van Brocklin may not have been the sort to see eye to eye with Tarkenton, but Grant was. Upon hearing that Tarkenton was available, he had told general manager Jim Finks, "He is the one quarterback I want for this team."[52] Tarkenton did not disappoint his coach. He put together a solid season in 1972, completing nearly 57 percent of his passes for 2,651 yards and eighteen touchdowns.

Unfortunately, that first year the Vikings were not able to capitalize on Tarkenton's talents. Several Vikings had gone through difficult salary negotiations during the off-season, and bitterness had developed between the players and management. Then, once the regular season got underway, the team was hit by a string of injuries to key players. As a consequence, the Vikings finished with a disappointing 7-7 record. Although Tarkenton was still voted the club's most valuable player by fans, the award did not lessen his frustration. "I'm the quarterback who was supposed to provide leadership," he said, "help this team win the Super Bowl. I don't want to belittle the award, but the only award that's meaningful is the one they give after the Super Bowl. This has to be my biggest disappointment of a lot of disappointments."[53]

Super Disappointments

In 1973, Tarkenton compiled the highest passer rating of his career (93.2) while completing nearly 62 percent of his throws. The Vikings won twelve of their fourteen regular season contests, then defeated the Redskins and Cowboys for the National Foot-

Tarkenton makes a handoff. In 1973 Tarkenton returned to Minnesota and led the Vikings to the Super Bowl.

ball Conference (NFC) title. They moved on to Super Bowl VIII, where their opponents were the defending Super Bowl champion Miami Dolphins.

Although Tarkenton felt confident about his team's chances, on this day the Dolphins were the better club. They jumped out to a 17-0 lead at halftime and went on to a 24-7 victory. For his part, Tarkenton completed a Super Bowl–record eighteen of twenty-eight passes for 166 yards and had only one interception.

The Vikings made it back to football's ultimate game the following season, after winning their sixth division title in seven years. This time their opponents were the Pittsburgh Steelers. The Steelers dominated play after halftime, and the result was another Minnesota loss, this time by a score of 16-6.

In 1977 Tarkenton lost his fourth Super Bowl, this time to the Oakland Raiders. The quarterback played two more seasons before retiring.

After a year's hiatus, Minnesota returned to the Super Bowl for the third time in four seasons on January 9, 1977. Their 11-2-1 record in the regular season was the best in the NFC. Tarkenton was ranked third in passing in the conference, after having topped the NFC the previous year.

Minnesota's opponents in Super Bowl XI were the Oakland Raiders. The Vikings were optimistic about their chances for victory. Unfortunately for Tarkenton's hopes for a Super Bowl ring, the Raiders defeated the Vikings, 32-14, in surprisingly easy fashion.

The Legacy

Tarkenton played two more seasons, guiding the Vikings to two more Central Division titles. The team came up short of the Super Bowl, however, despite his best efforts. In his final season of 1978, he set NFL single-season records for passes attempted (572) and completed (345), while leading the league with a career best 3,468 passing yards.

At the time of his retirement at age thirty-eight, Tarkenton had passed for more yards (47,003) and more touchdowns (342) than anyone who had ever played the game. His 6,467 attempted passes and 3,686 completions were also league records. Tarkenton is stung by the fact that many people prefer to dwell on his three Super Bowl losses. "It is the ultimate humiliation," said Tarkenton. "There is no consolation of any kind. People ridicule and abuse you. They look much more kindly on teams that don't get there than they do on a team that gets there . . . and loses."[54]

Tarkenton played eighteen seasons in the NFL and was remarkably injury free. He played in every one of his team's games in fourteen of those seasons and missed just one on three other occasions. Tarkenton's endurance record is all the more impressive in light of how opposing players reacted to his scrambling. Defensive players get frustrated and embarrassed when they try to run down a scrambling quarterback and fail. On the occasions when they finally do catch the quarterback, they have a tendency to take out their frustration by tackling even harder than normal. The fact that Tarkenton missed only nine games in his career is a testament to his physical toughness.

After his retirement, Tarkenton turned his attention to the business world. His motivation, mental toughness, and determination helped him there as it had on the football field. Over the years, he started more than a dozen successful companies. He also was a football commentator on television for ABC and a cohost of the television series *That's Incredible!*

Tarkenton is a millionaire several times over. He has coauthored several books on business and motivation. When most people think of him, however, it is as a scrambling quarterback, dodging tacklers to buy time until one of his receivers gets open. He may not have won a championship, but he paved the way for future quarterbacks who did, like Steve Young. His improvisational style and ability to bring out the best in his team were the reasons Bud Grant, his former coach with the Vikings, once said, "He's the greatest quarterback ever to play the game."[55]

CHAPTER 5

Joe Namath: The Symbol

In 1969, Joe Namath shocked the football world by leading the New York Jets to victory over the Baltimore Colts in Super Bowl III, a game that was instrumental in bringing about the merger between the upstart American Football League and the older, established National Football League. The brash youth who would earn the nickname "Broadway Joe" was one of the most colorful athletes of his day. His rifle arm and brash, bold, confident manner set him apart from other quarterbacks.

Growing Up in Beaver Falls

Born on May 31, 1943, in Beaver Falls, Pennsylvania, Joseph William Namath was the fourth son—and fifth child—of Frank and Rose Namath. Frank was a steelworker, as were many in the small town twenty-eight miles northwest of Pittsburgh. The family lived in a primarily African American section of Beaver Falls known as the Lower End. Young Joe, therefore, had both white and black playmates—a somewhat unusual circumstance in a time when segregation was widely practiced.

Joe was a natural athlete who took to sports at an early age. When he was five years old, he was introduced to football by his brothers, John, Robert, and Franklin. Rose Namath recalled:

> Bobby and Franklin always got up football games in the front yard. Joe was just five and too little to play, but the boys needed a quarterback. So Joe was it. Bobby and Franklin taught Joe to throw the ball over the telephone wires. They agreed he shouldn't be tackled. Joe got so he could throw the ball out of sight and he could hit a stump forty yards away.[56]

Joe was short for his age, a fact that hindered him in playing quarterback in peewee football, since he was unable to see over his offensive linemen. A strong arm and sturdy legs, however,

Joe Namath played all three big team sports in high school, excelling in basketball, baseball, and football. Namath turned down offers from professional teams in order to go to college.

helped him hold his own against bigger opponents since he could set up farther back behind the line and still reach his receivers.

At Beaver Falls High School, Joe played all three major team sports. As a guard, he captained the basketball squad. He also excelled as an outfielder on the baseball diamond and was scouted by several major league teams. "I wanted to sign a baseball contract," recalled Joe. "I had offers from the Cincinnati Reds, the Chicago Cubs, and other teams. My mother wouldn't let me accept any of them because she wanted me to have an education."[57]

In football, Joe was quarterback on the Beaver Falls junior varsity team as a sophomore in 1958, and moved up to the varsity for the last game of the year. As a five-foot-ten-inch, 150-pound junior, Joe began the season as a backup. By the end of the year, he began to impress the team's new coach, Larry Bruno, with his confidence and daring.

About this time, Joe began to show an independent attitude and streak of rebelliousness. Once, while having his picture taken for an all-star basketball team, the photographer told him to remove his sunglasses. Joe refused. "Look, mister," he said, "if you want the picture, you'll take it with my glasses on."[58]

Namath shot up four inches and put on twenty-five pounds in the summer before his senior year. Bruno handed him the starting quarterback job (as well as that of punter), and Namath made the most of his chance. In the first game of the season, against Midland High School, Namath ran 60 yards for a touchdown on the second play of the game. He also scored on another run and completed seven of seventeen passes for 174 yards in Beaver Falls's 43-13 victory.

Namath completed 58 percent of his passes for the year (85 of 146), good for 1,564 yards and twelve touchdowns. He led an otherwise undistinguished Beaver Falls team to an undefeated season and as a result drew the attention of more than fifty colleges from around the country. Eventually, Namath accepted a scholarship from the University of Alabama. His coach there would be the legendary Paul "Bear" Bryant.

Crimson Tide Star

That first year, Namath had trouble fitting in at Alabama. One difficulty Namath experienced was his white teammates' disapproval of the friendships he formed with blacks on the team. Namath, having grown up in a primarily African American neighborhood, was unprepared for such attitudes. Furthermore, Namath's tendency to wear flashy clothes and sport long hair stood out on the conservative southern campus. He even considered leaving Alabama after his freshman year, but Bryant talked him into staying around.

Namath began his sophomore year as the starting quarterback on a squad that had not been picked by sportswriters in the preseason to do well. In his first game as a starter, he tied a school record by throwing three touchdown passes to lead the Crimson Tide to a 35-0 win over what was supposedly a tough University of Georgia team. With Namath leading the way, the surprising Alabama squad compiled a 9-1 record and earned an invitation to the Orange Bowl. There, they shut out Oklahoma State University, 17-0, as Namath completed nine passes for eighty-six yards and one touchdown.

As a junior, Namath had another solid season. Following a loss to Auburn University late in the year, however, he was caught breaking one of coach Bryant's strict training rules (reportedly, the rule against drinking). He was suspended for the last game of the regular season and the Sugar Bowl. Bryant accepted part of the blame for the incident himself. "I knew Joe wasn't a bad boy," he later said. "I don't think he became bigheaded and felt he was above training rules. . . . I feel if I'd done a good job of leadership, the suspension wouldn't have happened."[59]

Namath learned his lesson and returned for his senior season with renewed determination. As teammate Galen McCullough told the *National Observer*, "He was a real leader . . . for the first time. Before, he used to just do his job and expect everyone else to do theirs. But this year he was always after everybody to do better."[60]

In the very first game of the season, Namath completed sixteen of twenty-one passes for 167 yards in leading Alabama to a 31-3 win over Georgia. Over the next two weeks, he guided his team to shutout wins over Tulane University and Vanderbilt University. While playing North Carolina State University in the fourth game of the year, however, Namath suffered an injury to his right knee while making a cut. Fluid was drained from the joint, but the injury severely restricted his movement.

Despite the injury, Namath completed sixty-four of one hundred passes for the season and led Alabama into the Orange Bowl. Unfortunately for Namath, in practice the week before the Orange Bowl his knee gave out and he was unable to start. However, when Alabama fell behind, 14-0, to the University of Texas, Namath entered the game and proceeded to complete an Orange Bowl–record eighteen of thirty-seven passes for 255 yards and a pair of touchdowns. Texas held on to win, 23-17, but Namath was voted the game's most valuable player in what some sportswriters called one of the gutsiest performances they had ever seen.

Namath's heroics were witnessed by Sonny Werblin, owner of the New York Jets of the American Football League. They had selected Namath in the first round of their draft on November 28, 1964, as had the St. Louis Cardinals of the older, more established National Football League. Werblin, the former president of MCA records, could see that Namath had immense potential, not just as a football player, but as something more. "Namath has the presence of a star," said Werblin. "You know how a real star lights up a room when he comes in. Joe has that quality."[61]

For his part, Namath thought the Jets could offer more money than the Cardinals and the chance to play in the media capital of

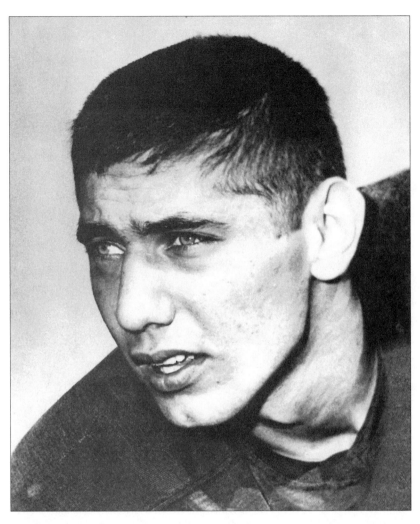

A legendary quarterback at the University of Alabama, Joe Namath led the team to one national championship game. After college, he went on to play for the New York Jets.

the world. On January 2, 1965—the day after the Orange Bowl—Werblin announced that the Jets had signed Namath to a three-year, $427,000 contract, at the time the largest in pro football history. Namath was on his way to New York City.

Broadway Joe

Upon coming to New York and the Jets, Namath was quick to let his teammates know what his priorities were. As offensive tackle Winston Hill remembered, "When Joe got here, he told us that he got all the money he could and he assumed we all did as well as

Namath attracted media attention for his many girlfriends and late-night partying. On the football field, he was the consummate professional.

we could too. He said he didn't want to hear about the money. If anyone wanted to fight him, he'd go outside with them, but inside or on the field he just wanted to win."[62]

Namath's signing did more than just improve the Jets' chances for success on the field. It immediately boosted the attention paid to the AFL. His first exhibition game, on July 28, 1965, in Lowell, Massachusetts, drew more sportswriters than had covered the league's championship game the year before.

Namath's lucrative contract also spurred a heated competition between the two leagues for the top college players, which resulted in an increase in players' salaries. In order to avoid an all-out war for players that would have raised salaries even more, the two leagues eventually agreed on a merger that would go into effect in 1970.

When Namath made his regular season debut in the second game of the year, on September 18, 1965, a record crowd of

53,658 filled New York's Shea Stadium. With the Jets trailing the Kansas City Chiefs by a score of 7-3, Namath entered the game and threw his first pass for a touchdown to end Don Maynard. He finished the day with eleven completions in twenty-three attempts for 121 yards. Although New York could not pull out the win, the fans had a new hero. They quickly came to love Namath's flamboyant style, his rifle arm, and his boyish charm.

That first season, Namath proceeded to lead the Jets to a second-place finish with a 5-8-1 mark. He compiled 2,220 yards passing and eighteen touchdown tosses for the season, and was named the AFL's rookie of the year. That January, Namath represented the Jets in the AFL All-Star Game against the champion Buffalo Bills. With the All-Stars losing at halftime, 13-6, Namath came back to throw for two touchdowns and lead his team to a 30-19 victory.

Off the field, Namath attracted constant media attention with his long hair, beautiful girlfriends, Upper East Side penthouse apartment, and late-night partying. Some criticized Namath's behavior, but as he explained in an interview in *Sports Illustrated* magazine, "I feel that everything I do is O.K. for me and doesn't affect anyone else, including the girls I go out with. Look man, I live and let live. I like everybody."[63] Rather than moderate his lifestyle, Namath became a fixture at New York's most popular night spots and soon acquired the nickname, first used by teammate Sherman Plunkett, of "Broadway Joe."

A Fast-Rising Star

Namath and the Jets got off to a fast start in 1966. The team won four of its first five games to move into first place in the AFL's Eastern Division. They slumped after that, however, and finished in third place with a record of 6-6-2. Still, Namath had an outstanding year, leading the league in pass attempts, completions, and passing yardage. The numbers he posted were even more amazing since he played most of the year with torn cartilage in his knee.

After undergoing surgery during the off-season, Namath began 1967 wearing a knee brace. It did not seem to hinder his performance, and he put together arguably the best season of his career. In leading the Jets to an 8-5-1 record and second-place finish in the AFL, Namath posted career highs in pass attempts (491), pass completions (258), touchdown passes (26), and passing yardage (4,007—the first time any pro quarterback reached the 4,000-yard plateau). By this time, the entire pro football world had begun to sit up and take notice of the strong-armed kid from Beaver Falls.

Super Bowl III and the Prediction

In the 1968 season, Namath led the Jets to an 11-3 record and their first AFL Eastern Division title. They moved on to New York, where they faced the Oakland Raiders in the league's championship game to determine who would play the NFL champion Baltimore Colts in Super Bowl III.

From the very beginning, Namath absorbed punishment that would have sidelined many quarterbacks. The Jets jumped out to a 10–0 lead over Oakland in the first quarter, but Namath sprained the thumb on his throwing hand. In the next period, he severely dislocated his left ring finger when he was hit by a pair of Oakland players. Just before halftime, Raiders Ike Lassiter and Ben Davidson barreled into Namath, knocking him to the ground with a concussion.

Somehow, Namath was back in the game when the second half started. When the dust finally settled, the Jets had won by a score of 27-23. Namath's three touchdown passes had led the team to its first AFL championship. The Jets moved on to Miami, Florida, where the Baltimore Colts awaited them.

The NFL was widely considered the stronger league. In the first two Super Bowls, the NFL's Green Bay Packers had defeated the Kansas City Chiefs and the Oakland Raiders respectively. The New York Jets were expected to do no better against the Baltimore Colts.

Namath, however, had no doubts about his or the Jets' prospects. Three days before the game, he made a brash prediction: "We're going to win Sunday," he said. "I guarantee you."[64]

Namath's boast made headlines in the sports section of newspapers across the country. That Sunday—January 12, 1969—with 75,377 fans in attendance at the Orange Bowl and nearly 60 million more at home watching on television, Namath backed up his words by leading the Jets to one of the biggest upsets in pro football history, beating Baltimore by a score of 16-7. Namath was named the contest's most valuable player by *Sport* magazine and awarded a new Dodge Charger. The game proved that the best teams in the new circuit could play on an equal basis with the best teams in the older, more established NFL. For his part, Namath's performance in Super Bowl III brought him a tremendous amount of publicity. He became more of a celebrity than ever, hobnobbing with movie stars and other entertainers and escorting beautiful young women to one party after another. Never one to avoid the public's eye, he chronicled many of his adventures in his autobi-

Joe Namath throws a pass in Super Bowl III in 1969. Despite several injuries, Namath and the Jets won the game.

ography, published that year, entitled *I Can't Wait Until Tomorrow . . . 'Cause I Get Better Looking Every Day.*

Some of Namath's adventures threatened to end his football career prematurely. One such misstep concerned an East Side bar in which he had invested called Bachelors III. Football commissioner Pete Rozelle claimed the club was frequented by gamblers—a serious allegation, since players were forbidden from associating with such individuals. He ordered Namath to sell his interests in the club or face indefinite suspension from football. Namath responded by announcing his retirement at age twenty-six. Before

Joe Namath signs autographs in New York. Namath's popularity began to wane after his victory in Super Bowl III.

the new season began, however, he reconsidered and sold his stake in the club.

Injuries Take Their Toll

Namath quickly found that glory in the NFL could be fleeting. He continued to lead the Jets over the next eight seasons, but he never again reached the heights attained in his first four years. He did lead the NFL in passing yardage and touchdown passes in 1972, but injuries severely limited his effectiveness. Included among his afflictions were a fractured wrist, a separated shoulder, and knee problems that required four operations.

As a result of his many injuries, Namath's pain was constant. His knees had to be drained of fluid before every game and iced down afterward. He never complained, however, exhibiting a courage that was marveled at by teammates and opponents alike. One such person was George Young, former general manager of the New York Giants. Remembering the exact day he became a Namath convert, Young recalled a 1974 game between the two New York teams. Young said:

> I never really cared for Namath, but he called a naked bootleg around left end. Well, everybody went right and he sort of limped into the end zone for the points that tied the score. He looked like a guy with two wooden legs. I had never realized how bad his knees were, but you could

really see it from the press box. It was like slow motion. It took a lot of courage to play with that.[65]

The Party Finally Ends

By 1976, Namath was just a shell of the player he had once been. Appearing in eleven games for the 3-11 Jets, his effectiveness had dropped precipitously. In compiling the lowest passer rating of his career (39.9), he tossed just four touchdown passes; worse, he

Joe Namath ended his legendary football career in 1977. He was inducted into the Professional Football Hall of Fame in 1985.

threw sixteen interceptions. Namath was eventually benched by coach Lou Holtz and then finally released. He signed with the Los Angeles Rams as a free agent and played four games for the team in 1977 before retiring.

After hanging up his cleats, Namath became involved in several other enterprises. He had been appearing in films since 1969. In 1978, he had a role in the short-lived television series, *The Waverly Wonders*. Namath has also worked as an analyst for NBC Sports and ABC's *Monday Night Football*.

Namath appeared in five All-Star games and counted the Hickock Belt for Professional Athlete of the Year, the George Halas Award for Most Courageous Athlete, and the Dodge Man of the Year Award among his trophies. In 1985, he was inducted into the Professional Football Hall of Fame.

Although there have been quarterbacks who have compiled better numbers, few have made as lasting an impression on the game of football as Namath. Former Jets owner Sonny Werblin put him in exclusive company. "Some people are bigger than life," said Werblin. "Babe Ruth. Clark Gable. Frank Sinatra. So is Joe Namath."[66]

CHAPTER 6

Joe Montana: The Coolest

Joe Montana ran San Francisco 49ers coach Bill Walsh's West Coast offense to perfection, leading the team to four Super Bowl titles. Montana's ability to come through under pressure earned him the nickname "Joe Cool." Perhaps no other quarterback better exhibited the ability to concentrate and get the job done when there is no margin for error than Joe Montana.

A Football Hotbed

Joseph Clifford Montana Jr. was born in the western Pennsylvania coal-mining town of New Engle on June 11, 1956, the only child of Joseph Sr. and Theresa Montana. Joe's father was a manager for the Civic Finance Company in nearby Monongahela. His mother was a secretary with the same firm.

Sports were an honored tradition in the Montana clan. Joe Jr.'s grandfather, Hooks Montana, had played semipro football in the 1920s, and Joe Sr. himself was a fervent fan. He encouraged his son to participate in sports of all kinds. For example, when his son was just eight months old, Joe Sr. gave him a bat and ball. He put up a hoop in the family's backyard so that Joe could play basketball, and he hung a tire so that Joe could practice throwing footballs through it. The boy showed enough talent that his father quit a job that required travel so that he could stay home and coach his son.

Joe Sr.'s coaching paid off. Young Joe played peewee football and Little League baseball and starred in both. He believed his early exposure to competition helped him later in his career. "Maybe it's because ever since I was little I was involved in pressure situations plus winning traditions," he recalled years later. "You knew you had to win, and you'd deal with it."[67]

At Ringgold High School in Monongahela, Joe was a pitcher on the baseball team, a guard on the basketball squad, a high jumper on the track-and-field team, and a quarterback in football. His football talent was obvious right from the beginning. "Joe was

San Francisco 49ers quarterback Joe Montana played college football at Notre Dame. Known for his calm and collected character, Montana was nicknamed "Joe Cool."

born to be a quarterback," said his high school quarterback coach, Jeff Petrucci. "You saw it in the midget leagues, in high school—the electricity in the huddle when he was in there."[68]

Joe's all-around athletic ability brought him to the attention of college sports recruiters throughout the country. He even had the opportunity to play basketball at North Carolina State University. Montana, however, wanted to attend Notre Dame University. "My father wanted me to go there," he explained, "and he had done so much for me throughout my early career that I didn't want to disappoint him."[69] So when Notre Dame at the last minute offered him a football scholarship, he quickly accepted.

The Birth of a Legend

Notre Dame was a disappointment at first. There were seven quarterbacks on the football powerhouse's freshman team in 1974. With such stiff competition, Montana played very little and began to get discouraged. The following year, Dan Devine took over from Ara Parseghian as head coach of the varsity team. The switch meant that Montana would have a better chance of starting, since Devine held an open competition for all jobs rather than just retaining those who had started for Parseghian. Montana performed well during spring practice and solidified his spot on the team.

Montana did not get a chance to play until the third game of the year against Northwestern University, when starter Rick Slager got hurt. With Notre Dame losing 7-0, Montana entered the game and led his team to a 31-7 win. The following week, however, Montana was back on the bench.

Montana got his next chance two weeks later against the University of North Carolina (UNC). UNC was leading 14-6 in the last quarter. Montana came in and led the Fighting Irish to a pair of touchdowns in just over a minute for a 21-14 victory.

Later that year, Montana directed his club to an even more unlikely win. With the Fighting Irish losing to the Air Force Academy, 30-10, Devine sent Montana into the game in the second half. Montana threw three touchdown passes in eight minutes to give Notre Dame a thrilling 31-30 triumph.

It was games such as these that earned Montana the nickname "Comeback Kid." No matter how wide the margin by which Notre Dame was losing, Montana had a knack for rallying his team to put together an improbable win. Though other quarterbacks may have been more impressive physical specimens, Montana seemed to be able to do whatever was necessary to guide his team to victory.

Montana proved that he could save games for Notre Dame, but his hopes of starting for the Irish in 1976 were dashed when he suffered a separated shoulder in the last preseason scrimmage. The injury forced him to sit out the year as a redshirt. When Montana returned for his junior year, he began the season as the third-string quarterback.

Once again, Montana found himself coming off the bench to save an otherwise lost cause. In the third game of the year, against Purdue, with Notre Dame trailing, 24-14, he entered the game with two minutes left in the third period. Montana led the Irish back to victory.

The comeback against Purdue finally convinced Devine that Montana was worthy of being the starter. That decision proved the right one, as Notre Dame did not lose another game the rest of the season. They moved on to the Cotton Bowl, where they dismantled a strong University of Texas team, 38-10. By doing so, they finished the year as national champions.

Montana closed out his college career as a fifth-year senior in 1978. Although Notre Dame's record was just 8-3, Montana had his best year statistically. He completed 54.2 percent of his passes for 2,010 yards, both career highs. In his final college game, fighting the effects of the flu, he brought the Irish back from a 34-12 deficit against the University of Houston in the Cotton Bowl to earn a thrilling 35-34 win. He was named the game's most valuable player for his heroics, which included throwing the winning touchdown pass on the final play of the game.

Making Believers of the Pros

Despite Montana's heroics at Notre Dame, many NFL teams did not believe he possessed the physical skills to succeed in the pros. The San Francisco 49ers, however, felt differently, seeing real ability in addition to his intangible leadership qualities. As new head coach Bill Walsh later explained:

> People who say [his is] only an average arm are mistaken. And they always will be. Because his delivery is not a flick of the wrist like [Pittsburgh Steelers quarterback] Terry Bradshaw's, they think it's not strong. He throws on the run while avoiding a pass rush, and he does not have to be totally set. He is not a moving platform like some others who are mechanical and can only do well when everything is just right. Joe performs just as well under stress.[70]

Despite the team's obvious need for new talent (they had won only two games the previous season), Walsh decided to bring Montana along slowly. "Joe had some advantages," said his coach. "He was in a situation where there wasn't much pressure on him because nobody expected him to win. He could watch and learn from Steve DeBerg, who was a very good quarterback. He had people like [wide receiver] Dwight Clark who could make big plays." [71] The rookie made brief appearances in all sixteen of the team's games, but threw a total of just twenty-three passes all year.

Montana earned the respect of the NFL as a 49er quarterback with his knack for inspiring his teammates to come from behind and win.

One of Montana's biggest advantages was having Walsh as his coach. Through the years, Walsh had played a major role in the development of talented quarterbacks such as Virgil Carter, Greg Cook, Kenny Anderson, and Dan Fouts, all of whom had had successful pro careers. He was the architect of what became known as the West Coast offense, a system based on a short-passing game that would fit Montana's style perfectly.

The next season, Montana began to see more and more action. Once again, Montana's ability to inspire his teammates to come from behind worked to his benefit. On December 7, 1980, he rallied the 49ers back from a twenty-eight-point halftime deficit, guiding them to an incredible 38-35 overtime victory over the New Orleans Saints. At the time, it was the greatest comeback in NFL history. "That was really Joe's breakout game," said Walsh. "That gave him the confidence he could do the job."[72] From that point on, the starting position was his.

The Road to the Championship

San Francisco finished the 1980 season with a record of 6-10. That summer, the 49ers traded DeBerg to the Denver Broncos, a move that showed their commitment to Montana. "Steve was such a charismatic leader," said Walsh, "such a competitor, that I don't think Joe could ever have become the leader we needed with him around."[73] The twenty-five-year-old Montana began to feel more relaxed and comfortable in this role, and it showed on the field.

After losing their first two games in 1981, the 49ers won thirteen of their next fourteen. They defeated the Giants in the divisional play-off to advance to the NFC Championship Game. Their opponent would be the Dallas Cowboys.

Once again, the Comeback Kid worked his magic. With Dallas leading 27-21 with four minutes and nineteen seconds left to play, Montana took the 49ers downfield from their own eleven-yard line to the Dallas six. There, on third down with just fifty-eight seconds remaining, Montana spied Dwight Clark in the corner of the end zone. Just before getting hit, Montana released the ball. Extending himself to his full height, Clark caught the ball for the touchdown that gave San Francisco the victory. "The Cowboys said Joe was trying to throw the ball away," said Walsh, "but that was a designed play. That and the drive were typical of Joe. We worked in practice on those situations, and Joe performed in the game exactly as he practiced."[74] The play, which became known simply as "The Catch," sent the 49ers to the Super Bowl for the first time in franchise history.

Super Bowl Hero

The 49ers' opponents in Super Bowl XVI were the Cincinnati Bengals, who were quarterbacked by another Bill Walsh disciple, Kenny Anderson. In the first half, Montana directed San Francisco on the longest scoring drive in Super Bowl history (92 yards) as the 49ers jumped out to a 20-0 lead. The Bengals fought back in the second half, but the 49ers held on to win, 26-21. Montana completed fourteen of twenty-two passes for 157 yards and was named the game's most valuable player. Modestly, he downplayed his performance and praised the contributions of kicker Ray Wersching and the San Francisco defense.

What Montana's teammates found particularly helpful in crucial games was his unflappable nature, a quality that earned him a new nickname, "Joe Cool." This ability to remain calm under the pressure of play-off games and the Super Bowl was nothing new to those who knew him from the past. In fact, following the Super Bowl, a former teammate of Montana's at Notre Dame, Cincinnati defensive end Ross Browner, recalled that college coach Devine had failed to see this aspect of Montana. "This was one of those games that showcased his talent. Joe just wasn't Dan Devine's type of quarterback. He was just too cool for Devine, too calm and collected. Joe had it in him all the time. Devine just didn't realize it."[75]

Despite Montana's efforts, San Francisco would not return to the Super Bowl for three years. In 1984, he had one of his greatest

Joe Montana dodges a Cincinnati Bengal tackle in Super Bowl XVI. In the first half of the game, Montana led the 49ers in the longest scoring drive in Super Bowl history.

seasons. Montana completed nearly 65 percent of his passes, threw for 3,630 yards, and had twenty-eight touchdown passes. The 49ers lost just one game during the regular season and shut out the Chicago Bears, 23-0, in the NFC Championship Game.

Super Bowl XIX was billed as a duel between the league's two top quarterbacks, Montana and Miami's Dan Marino, who had set league records for passing yardage and touchdown tosses. The outcome of the game, however, left no question as to who was number one. The 49ers demolished the Miami Dolphins by a score of 38-16 as Montana completed twenty-four of thirty-five passes

Montana in action during Super Bowl XIX. Montana led the 49ers to four Super Bowl victories.

for 331 yards and three touchdowns. He also ran for another score and won his second Super Bowl most valuable player trophy. Montana was praised by Miami defensive coordinator Chuck Studley, who said, "There's nobody else like him. . . . The way he knows where he is, where his receivers are, that complete vision he has—it's unbelievable."[76]

A Serious Injury and Doubts About the Future

It would be another three years before the 49ers returned to football's ultimate game. Montana continued to shine, throwing for 3,653 yards and twenty-seven touchdowns in 1985 before San Francisco fell to the Giants in the first round of the play-offs.

Montana's ability to stage amazing comebacks was severely tested on a personal level when he ruptured a disk in his back while throwing a pass in the opening game of the 1985 season. He underwent two hours of career-threatening surgery and was told by doctors that he would miss the entire season. Against all odds, he returned to action two months later to play against the St. Louis Cardinals. In an amazing comeback, Montana threw three touchdown passes to lead San Francisco to a 43-17 win over the Cardinals. Montana also maintained a positive outlook regarding his future, saying, "The doctor told me that of the people who had the surgery I had, seventy percent need surgery again down the line. It could be twenty years, it could be tomorrow. Hopefully, I'll be one of the thirty percent who don't need it at all. That's the way I approached it."[77] He helped his team win the NFC West title, but the Giants brought San Francisco's season to a close by defeating the 49ers in the first round of the play-offs.

Although Montana had bounced back from his surgery, many observers wondered how many last-minute heroics he had left in him. In the 1987 postseason, Montana had arguably the worst play-off game of his career in the opening round against the Minnesota Vikings. He threw for just 109 yards, was sacked four times, and had an interception returned for a touchdown. With the 49ers losing, 27-10, Montana was replaced by Steve Young in the third quarter, a move unappreciated by a number of his teammates. "When Joe was pulled from that Minnesota game," recalled Dwight Clark, "my comment was 'This is bull.' Here is the greatest comeback quarterback of all time. If anyone is going to pull it out, it's Joe."[78]

The Vikings held on to win, and many expressed doubts about Montana's football future. He would put them all to rest in 1988.

Back to the Super Bowl

Steve Young saw more playing time as Montana's understudy in 1988, and rumors began to surface that Montana might be traded. These only made him more determined than ever to prove he could still do the job. He did so by leading San Francisco to another Western Division title. Play-off wins against the Vikings and Chicago Bears put Montana and the 49ers back in the Super Bowl for a third time.

In Super Bowl XXIII, Montana once again performed his magic in pressure-packed circumstances. The Cincinnati Bengals led San Francisco, 16-13, with three minutes and twenty seconds left in the game. Starting on the 49ers' own eight-yard line, Montana guided them all the way downfield. With just thirty-four seconds remaining in the game, he tossed a ten-yard pass to wide receiver John Taylor for a touchdown that gave San Francisco a 20-16 victory. He finished with 23 completed passes for a Super Bowl–record 357 yards through the air. Said Montana, "It's got to be one of our best wins ever."[79]

At the age of thirty-three, Montana was determined to show that he was not yet through. The next year, he had arguably the greatest all-around season of his pro career for new coach George Seifert, who replaced the retired Walsh. Montana completed an incredible 70.2 percent of his passes for 3,521 yards and twenty-eight touchdowns.

Montana and the 49ers breezed through the postseason, defeating the Vikings, 41-13, in the divisional play-off and the Los Angeles Rams, 30-3, for the NFC championship. In the latter contest, Montana completed an amazing twenty-six of thirty passes for 262 yards and two touchdowns.

Playing in his fourth Super Bowl in nine years, Montana was magnificent. He completed twenty-two of twenty-nine passes for 297 yards and a Super Bowl–record five touchdowns in leading San Francisco to a 55-10 rout of the Denver Broncos, the most lopsided win in an NFL title game in forty-nine years. Montana won his third Super Bowl most valuable player award for his performance, becoming just the second quarterback ever (along with Terry Bradshaw of the Pittsburgh Steelers) to win four Super Bowls.

Montana had one more solid year for the 49ers. He threw for a career-high 3,944 yards in 1990 to lead San Francisco to a 14-2 record in the regular season. In the NFC Championship Game against the Giants, however, he broke his finger, a mishap that ended his season.

Winding Down a Memorable Career

Now, physical ailments took their toll on Montana. Montana injured his elbow during training camp in 1991 and had to have surgery. He missed the entire season as Young took over the starting job. He did not return to action until the final game of the 1992 campaign. By that time, Young had established himself as the 49ers' starting quarterback. Unwilling to return to the number two slot, Montana requested a trade and was sent to the Kansas City Chiefs in April 1993.

Montana went on to play for the Kansas City Chiefs before retiring in 1995. His career is marked above all by an ability to thrive under pressure.

Montana helped the Chiefs make the play-offs in 1993 and showed he still had some magic left in his arm. In Kansas City's first-round game against Pittsburgh, he threw a touchdown pass to tie the score with less than two minutes left in regulation time. The Chiefs went on to win in overtime. In the club's next game against the Houston Oilers, Montana threw a pair of touchdown passes in the last ten minutes to lead Kansas City to a 28-20 victory. His luck finally ended in the AFC Championship Game against the Buffalo Bills. Montana suffered a concussion and was forced to leave the game. The Chiefs lost by a score of 30-13.

Montana played one more season with Kansas City before announcing his retirement in April 1995. Since then, he has worked as an analyst for NBC television, run an East Coast sports bar, and been involved with running an auto racing team. He spends most of his time with his wife and four children and is planning a new venture: the Joe Montana Football Fantasy Camp. As he explained, "I want to teach football and mix it up. I miss football, and this gets me back into it. It's a different level, and I can at least dream of what I used to be."[80]

In fifteen NFL seasons, Montana won four Super Bowls, led the league in passing five times, was named All-NFL three times, and was voted to the Pro Bowl eight times. At the time of his retirement, he ranked fourth in career passing yardage, attempts, and touchdowns. He placed third in completions and second in career passer rating.

All these numbers, however, just begin to give an indication of Montana's value to his team. His composure and ability to handle pressure enabled him to bring his club back from last-quarter deficits to victory an incredible thirty-one times. As former teammate Randy Cross once said, "There have been, and will be, much better arms and legs and much better bodies on quarterbacks in the NFL, but if you have to win a game or score a touchdown or win a championship, the only guy to get is Joe Montana."[81]

CHAPTER 7

Dan Marino: The Arm

Dan Marino is generally considered to have been the best pure passer—that is, someone with the accuracy and arm strength to complete any type of pass on a consistent basis—ever. His height, quick release, and exceptional arm strength helped him set numerous single-season and career passing marks. Although Marino's Miami Dolphins never won a Super Bowl, Marino stands atop the NFL as the most prolific passer in league history.

Miami Dolphins quarterback Dan Marino throws a pass in a 1997 game. The star has been called the most prolific passer in the NFL.

The Streets of Pittsburgh

Daniel Constantine Marino Jr. was born on September 15, 1961. He was the first child—and only son—of Dan Sr. and Veronica Marino. Dan was born and raised in the South Oakland area of Pittsburgh, Pennsylvania, a middle-class Italian and Irish neighborhood populated by steelworkers, truck drivers, and laborers.

Dan Sr. was a truck driver who delivered newspapers on the midnight shift for the *Pittsburgh Post-Gazette*. His job did not pay a lot of money, but it allowed him to spend a good deal of time with his son. This was especially helpful to the maturation of Dan's athletic talents. "The biggest thing in my early development," recalled Dan, "is that my dad had a job where he could be home in the afternoon, waiting for me to get out of school. Then we would throw to each other the rest of the day."[82]

Young Dan loved all sports. Unfortunately, he did not have as much interest in his schoolwork. He attended a parochial school

Marino played as quarterback for the University of Pittsburgh. The Pennsylvania native brought his team to victory in the Fiesta and Sugar bowls.

across the street from his house called St. Regis, where he also was an altar boy. His grades there were so poor, his sixth-grade teacher did not think Dan would even be able to graduate from high school. The youngster's parents knew the problem had less to do with intelligence than with motivation, since he never seemed to have problems learning anything that had to do with sports.

Dan's parents encouraged him to study, stressing how academic failure might hurt his future in sports by keeping him from attending college. Dan worked hard, and his grades improved enough to enable him to gain admission to Central Catholic High School, known for developing its students' athletic talents.

At Central, Dan did well not just in football but in baseball as well. With a fastball that was clocked at ninety-two miles per hour and a .550 batting average, he was scouted by several major league teams. Dan was drafted by the Kansas City Royals in the fourth round of the June 1979 free agent draft and seriously considered signing, but eventually decided to stick with football, his first love.

Dan was a standout quarterback, placekicker, and punter on Central's football team. It was his strong arm that brought him to the attention of many of the nation's top college football programs. The nearby University of Pittsburgh began scouting him in his sophomore year and eventually offered him a scholarship. He also received offers from the University of California at Los Angeles, Michigan State University, Arizona State University, and Clemson University, among others. He eventually accepted the one from Pittsburgh so that he could remain close to home. As he later explained, "Something, maybe my heart, told me to stay home and go to Pitt."[83]

The Pittsburgh Panthers

Marino entered Pittsburgh in the fall of 1979 and almost immediately took over the starting quarterback job when the regular quarterback suffered a leg injury halfway through the season. The six-foot-four-inch freshman with the rifle arm and quick release led the Panthers to five straight wins, including a victory over Arizona in the postseason Fiesta Bowl. In guiding Pittsburgh to an 11-1 record, Marino finished tenth in the nation in the passing ratings compiled by the National Collegiate Athletic Association.

After helping Pittburgh to another 11-1 mark as a sophomore, Marino enjoyed his best college season in 1981 as a junior. He set school single-season records for completions (226), passing yards (2,876), and touchdown tosses (37) and was named All-America.

Marino capped his season by being named most valuable player in the Sugar Bowl, where he led the Panthers to a 24-20 victory over Georgia. Pittsburgh finished at 11-1 for the third straight year and held high hopes for the following season.

At the beginning of Marino's senior year, Pittsburgh was ranked number one by members of the media in the preseason polls. The year, however, was a disappointment as both the quarterback and his team failed to fulfill their potential (perhaps in part due to overconfidence). Marino's statistics fell off from the previous year, and Pittsburgh finished with a record of 9-3. Marino was also troubled by rumors of drug use. He tested negative, but the rumors continued.

If Marino's senior year was a disappointment for him, it proved to be good luck for the Miami Dolphins. When the NFL draft was held that June, Miami was the twenty-seventh team to pick. Ordinarily a player of Marino's stature would have been picked long before, but other clubs, apparently concerned about the drug rumors, passed Marino up. When Miami's turn came, Marino had not yet been taken. The Dolphins were thankful for their good fortune. "We just never thought Dan would be around when it was our turn to draft," said Miami head coach Don Shula. "I had always liked everything I saw in him, his mannerisms, his mechanics, especially his quick release. He was a heck of a quarterback to be out there on the twenty-seventh pick; a heck of a buy."[84]

An Exciting Rookie

Marino signed a four-year, $2-million contract with Miami and began his rookie season as backup to David Woodley, who had led the team to the Super Bowl the previous year. After a slow start in 1983, however, Shula decided a change was in order. With the Dolphins struggling against the Los Angeles Raiders, he replaced Woodley with Marino. The rookie connected on eleven of his seventeen passes, including two for touchdowns. Miami still lost by a score of 27-14, but everyone who witnessed Marino's debut was impressed.

After substituting for Woodley one more time, Marino made his first start three weeks later against the Buffalo Bills. The Dolphins lost in overtime, 38-35, but the rookie was spectacular. He completed nineteen of twenty-nine passes, good for 322 yards and three touchdowns, and even impressed Buffalo coach Kay Stephenson. "That Marino is going to be an excellent quarterback," said Stephenson. "Frankly, he did a lot more than I thought possible for a rookie."[85] From that point on, Marino was Miami's starting quarterback. He justified Shula's faith in him by leading the team to the AFC Eastern Division title.

Although the Dolphins were eliminated by the Seattle Seahawks in the first round of the play-offs, Marino led the conference in passing and was named rookie of the year. He was also selected to play in the Pro Bowl and became the first rookie quarterback to start in the game.

A Career Year

Marino changed the way football was played in Miami. Until 1983, the Dolphins had a reputation as a defensive team that controlled the tempo of the game by running the ball. Running backs like Larry Csonka, Mercury Morris, and Jim Kiick were the cornerstones of the teams of the early 1970s, together with defensive stalwarts like linebacker Nick Buoniconti. With Marino as quarterback, Shula was able to build an offense around the pass. Most of those who had doubts about the new approach were won over in 1984. In the very first game of the season, Marino led the Dolphins to a 35-17 win over the Washington Redskins. In the

Dan Marino enjoyed the greatest season ever for an NFL quarterback in 1983. But the glory faded when the Dolphins lost Super Bowl XIX to the 49ers.

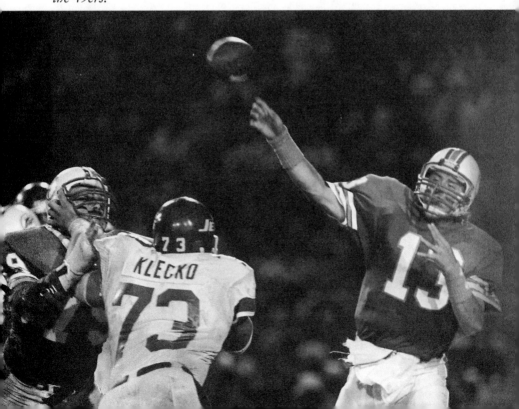

process, he completed twenty-one of twenty-eight passes for 311 yards, five touchdowns, and no interceptions. It was the beginning of what would be the greatest season ever put together by an NFL quarterback. The Dolphins won their first eleven games and breezed to a league-best record of 14-2. Marino set league single-season marks for completions (362), passing yardage (5,084), and touchdown passes (48). He threw for over 400 yards in a game on five separate occasions.

After beating Seattle in the AFC divisional play-offs, the Dolphins defeated the Steelers, 45-28, to take the conference championship. Marino set AFC Championship Game records with 421 passing yards and four touchdown passes. The win earned the Dolphins a spot in Super Bowl XIX against the San Francisco 49ers and their star quarterback, Joe Montana.

On Super Bowl Sunday, however, the 49ers clearly were the better team. San Francisco's defense kept putting pressure on Marino, and as a result, despite a Super Bowl–record fifty pass attempts, Marino and the Dolphins lost, 38-16. Although disappointed, the twenty-three-year-old made no excuses for his losing performance. "They played the best any team has played against us defensively," he said after the game. "They took us out of our scheme. . . . We knew what we had to do . . . and we didn't."[86]

Contract Negotiations

Despite the loss in the Super Bowl, Marino's performance in 1984 raised him to almost legendary status in the eyes of some observers. Pete Axthelm of *Newsweek* said, "Marino is not just what some coaches call an impact player, a man who drastically alters the personality of his team. He is a quantum-leap player who is changing the entire nature of his art."[87]

With such raves ringing in his ears, Marino tried to renegotiate his contract for 1985 in order to bring it in line with Montana's salary. Dolphins' owner Joe Robbie refused to agree to his demands, and Marino staged a thirty-seven-day holdout in training camp. He rejoined the team just prior to the start of the regular season and played under the terms of his existing contract, which still had two years to go.

For 1985, Marino did well but could not match the numbers compiled in his record-setting season. He still led the NFL in completions, passing yards, and touchdown passes in 1985 while helping the Dolphins to a 12-4 mark. As Greg Logan wrote in *Newsday*, "An 'off' year for Marino means he went from all-time to merely all-Pro."[88] Miami defeated the Browns in the divisional play-offs, but lost to the New England Patriots in the AFC Championship Game to fall short in their bid to return to the Super Bowl.

Marino resumed his pursuit of a new contract in the off-season. By August 1986, nothing more had been settled. Marino blasted Robbie in an interview that appeared in *Sport* magazine, but finally, in early September, the two sides managed to work out an agreement. Marino signed a lucrative new six-year contract worth $9 million.

Disappointments

New contract in hand, Marino continued to post solid numbers over the next three years. With wide receivers Mark Clayton and Mark Duper as his favorite targets, Marino led the AFC in passing yardage with 4,746 yards in 1986, the third-highest total in league history. His forty-four touchdown tosses—six of which came in a game against the Jets—were second only to his record forty-eight in 1984. In the strike-shortened 1987 season, he led the AFC in both completions and touchdown passes. In another game against the Jets the following year, he passed for 521 yards, the second-highest single-game total in NFL history.

The Dolphins, however, could not match their star's accomplishments. In the three-year span from 1986 to 1988, Miami finished with records of 8-8, 8-7, and 6-10 and failed to make the play-offs each year. The fault was not Marino's; a porous defense was the team's downfall.

It was a difficult 1989 season for Marino, when he posted the worst numbers of his career.

Miami's woes seemed to get the best of Marino in 1989. As the Dolphins plodded along to another mediocre 8-8 record, Marino struggled through the worst season of his career. He completed a career-low 56.0 percent of his passes while compiling a 76.9 passer rating (also a career low).

The Dolphins finally made it back to the play-offs in 1990. An improved defense allowed just fifteen points per game during the regular season. Marino threw the ball less often than in past years as the running game took on more of a role in the offense. The change in offensive philosophy did not bother Marino. "If it took me handing the ball off on every play for us to make the playoffs," he said, "I'd be thrilled to do that."[89] When the defense collapsed in the divisional play-offs against Buffalo, however, the Dolphins' season came to an abrupt halt.

The Elusive Championship

Prior to the start of the 1991 season, Marino signed a new five-year, $25-million contract that made him the highest-paid player in the game. When the Dolphins struggled to another 8-8 record and failed to make the play-offs, the quarterback naturally came in for a good bit of the blame from the fans.

Marino still posted good numbers, but he took more of a beating from opposing defenses. Poor blocking by the Miami defensive line allowed opposing players to sack him fifteen times in the first half of the season alone. In previous years, he had rarely been sacked, since his lightning-quick release usually allowed him to get rid of the ball before defenders reached him.

In succeeding years, Marino dealt with one frustration after another in his quest for the elusive championship. He led the NFL in completions and passing yardage for the fifth time in 1992, but the Buffalo Bills stopped the Dolphins in the AFC Championship Game with the aid of a potent rushing game.

The next year, Marino suffered a torn right Achilles tendon in the fifth game of the year. Up to that point, he had been the most durable quarterback in the league, having played in an NFL-high 145 consecutive games. The Dolphins lost their last five games of the regular season with him out of the lineup and missed making the play-offs.

A subpar preseason in 1994 caused some observers to question Marino's ability to bounce back from his injury. He quickly put such doubts to rest and went on to have one of the greatest seasons of his career. Marino completed 62.6 percent of his passes for 4,453 yards and thirty touchdowns in leading Miami to the AFC

Eastern Division title. In the second round of the play-offs, however, the Dolphins blew a 21-6 lead to the San Diego Chargers and lost by a score of 22-21.

In 1995, Marino moved to the top of the NFL career listings in most passing categories. He set career marks for passing attempts, completions, passing yardage, and touchdown passes. Still, he got little satisfaction from setting the records. As he explained, "Football is a team game, and losing takes away from the records. Every record I've set has been in a game we've lost. It's hard to appreciate them."[90]

The Dolphins made a quick exit from the play-offs with a first-round loss, and head coach Don Shula announced his retirement. It remained for Miami's new coach, former Dallas Cowboys head coach Jimmy Johnson, to try to get Marino his Super Bowl ring.

The Johnson Years

Johnson had been successful at both the University of Miami (winning a national title in 1987) and with the Cowboys (winning Super Bowls in 1992 and 1993). He expected no less in Miami. "I'd be disappointed," he said, "if we didn't win a title within three years."[91] One of the first moves in his plan was to sign Marino to a new three-year, $17.9 million contract.

Unfortunately for Marino, Johnson could not work his magic with the Dolphins. Miami made the play-offs in each of the next three seasons (1997, 1998, and 1999) but could not make it back to the conference championship game. In 1999, the Dolphins lost to the Jacksonville Jaguars, 62-7, in the AFC divisional play-offs, a game Marino called the ugliest he ever played because of his—and his team's—poor performance.

The Jacksonville game convinced Miami management that the thirty-eight-year-old Marino was no longer capable of being a starting quarterback. He had missed five games during the regular season because of injuries and had finished the year with more interceptions than touchdown passes for the only time in his seventeen-year career.

Convinced he still could play, Marino became a free agent and was contacted by three teams. He seriously considered playing for the Minnesota Vikings in one last attempt at winning a championship, but ultimately decided against it. "In the end," he explained, "the physical part of it was going to be hard. Minnesota plays, I think, 11 games on artificial turf this year, which would be tough on my legs. It was going to be hard on my wife and kids, too. In this day and age, especially with the relationship I've built

Dan Marino retired holding nearly every career passing record in the history of the NFL. Despite never winning a Super Bowl, Marino carries a total of 147 victories.

with this community, I didn't think it'd be right to go somewhere else for a year."[92] His ties to the community include the Dan Marino Foundation in Weston, Florida, which helps children with chronic illnesses and developmental disabilities, and the Toyota Dan Marino Celebrity Invitational golf tournament he holds annually at Weston Hills Country Club to raise money for youth charities.

A Future Hall of Famer

Marino retired as the most prolific passer in the history of professional football. He holds nearly every career passing record by wide margins, including most pass attempts (8,358—1,891 more than Fran Tarkenton in second place), completions (4,967—1,281 more than Tarkenton), touchdown passes (420—78 more than Tarkenton), and total yards passing (61,361—14,361 more than Tarkenton). Among his other marks are most four-thousand-yard seasons (6), most four-touchdown games (19), and most consecutive play-off games with a touchdown pass (12).

Observers widely agree that Marino will be elected to the Professional Football Hall of Fame as soon as he becomes eligible. Despite the fact that he never won a Super Bowl, he was a winner nonetheless with his career total of 147 victories second only to John Elway's 148. He will always be remembered for terrorizing opposing defenses as the most feared passer ever. As former Redskins quarterback Joe Theismann said, "What Marino did with the Dolphins sort of revolutionized football. He really transformed the game into an exciting aerial show in Miami."[93]

Marino continues to live with his family in South Florida. He currently works as a commentator for the *Inside the NFL* series on HBO.

NOTES

Introduction: The Toughest Position in Sports
  1. Quoted in Peter King, *Greatest Quarterbacks*. New York: Time, 1999, p. 10.
  2. Quoted in King, *Greatest Quarterbacks*, p. 154.

Chapter 1: Sammy Baugh: The Revolutionary
  3. Quoted in Andy Friedlander, "Sammy Baugh," *Dallas-Fort Worth Star Telegram*, September 29, 2002. www.drw.com.
  4. Quoted in "One Hundred Greatest Players of All-Time: Number Three Sammy Baugh," *College Football News*. www.collegefootballnews.com.
  5. Quoted in Jan Reid, "Legends of the Fall," *Texas Monthly*, November 1997.
  6. Quoted in Mickey Herskowitz, *The Quarterbacks*. New York: William Morrow, 1990, p. 24.
  7. Quoted in Herskowitz, *The Quarterbacks*, p. 25.
  8. Quoted in Larry Schwartz, "Baugh Perfected the Perfect Pass," *ESPN*. www.espn.go.com.
  9. Quoted in Dennis Tuttle, "Still Slingin'," *Sporting News*, November 7, 1994, p. 12.
  10. Quoted in "Baugh Suspects 1940 Redskins Threw Title Game to Spite Owner," *Amarillo Globe-News*, November 28, 1999.
  11. Quoted in Schwartz, "Baugh Perfected the Perfect Pass."
  12. Quoted in Peter King, *Football: A History of the Professional Game*. New York: Time, 1996, p. 116.
  13. Quoted in Tuttle, "Still Slingin'," p. 12.
  14. Quoted in Herskowitz, *The Quarterbacks*, p. 29.
  15. Quoted in John McFarland, "Hall of Famer Sammy Baugh Reflects Fifty Years After Career Ended," *Yahoo!* www.ca.yahoo.com.
  16. Quoted in Noel Epstein, ed., *Redskins: A History of Washington's Team*. Washington, DC: Washington Post Books, 1997, p. 41.

Chapter 2: Otto Graham: The Winner

17. Quoted in Bob Carroll et al., eds., *Total Football*. New York: HarperCollins, 1997, p. 429.

18. Walter Paulison, *The Tale of the Wildcats*. Chicago: Northwestern University Club of Chicago, 1951.

19. Paulison, *The Tale of the Wildcats*.

20. Quoted in King, *Football,* p. 104.

21. Quoted in Larry Schwartz, "'Automatic Otto' Defined Versatility," *ESPN.* www.espn.go.com.

22. Quoted in Paul Zimmerman, "Revolutionaries," *Sports Illustrated*, August 17, 1998, p. 81.

23. Quoted in King, *Greatest Quarterbacks*, p. 19.

24. Quoted in Zimmerman, "Revolutionaries," p. 82.

25. Quoted in "Graham's Legend Told Through Stories," *Mansfield News Journal*, November 4, 2002.

26. Quoted in "Otto Graham: He Was the Man," *NFL History Network.* www.nflhistory.net.

27. Quoted in Schwartz, "'Automatic Otto' Defined Versatility."

Chapter 3: Johnny Unitas: The Battler

28. Johnny Unitas and Ed Fitzgerald, *The Johnny Unitas Story*. New York: Grosset and Dunlap, 1968, p. 23.

29. Quoted in Unitas and Fitzgerald, *The Johnny Unitas Story*, p. 24.

30. Quoted in Zimmerman, "Revolutionaries," p. 82.

31. Quoted in Herskowitz, *The Quarterbacks*, p. 92.

32. Quoted in "Unitas Dies of Heart Attack at Sixty-Nine," *NFL.* www.nfl.com.

33. Quoted in Herskowitz, *The Quarterbacks*, p. 94.

34. Quoted in Zimmerman, "Revolutionaries," p. 82.

35. Quoted in "Unitas' Star Rose After Yankee Stadium Heroics," *ESPN.* www.espn.co.com.

36. Quoted in King, *Greatest Quarterbacks,* p. 31.

37. Quoted in Herskowitz, *The Quarterbacks*, pp. 97–98.

38. Quoted in "Unitas Dies of Heart Attack at Sixty-Nine."

39. Quoted in Herskowitz, *The Quarterbacks*, p. 104.

40. Quoted in "Unitas Was Original, Incredible," *NFL*. www.nfl.com.

Chapter 4: Fran Tarkenton: The Scrambler

41. Quoted in Herskowitz, *The Quarterbacks*, p. 144.

42. Quoted in Shane Hannon, "Legends: Fran Tarkenton," *Online Athens*. www.onlineathens.com.

43. Quoted in Hannon, "Legends."

44. Jim Klobuchar and Fran Tarkenton, *Tarkenton*. New York: Harper and Row, 1976, p. 42.

45. Quoted in *Georgia Dogs*. www.georgiadogs.ocsn.com.

46. Quoted in Herskowitz, *The Quarterbacks*, p. 145.

47. Quoted in Herskowitz, *The Quarterbacks*, p. 146.

48. Quoted in Beau Riffenburgh and David Boss, *Great Ones*. New York: Viking Penguin, 1989, p. 25.

49. Quoted in King, *Greatest Quarterbacks*, p. 107.

50. Klobuchar and Tarkenton, *Tarkenton*, p. 149.

51. Quoted in Herskowitz, *The Quarterbacks*, p. 147.

52. Quoted in Herskowitz, *The Quarterbacks*, p. 164.

53. Quoted in Herskowitz, *The Quarterbacks*, p. 167.

54. Quoted in Herskowitz, *The Quarterbacks*, p. 144.

55. Quoted in King, *Greatest Quarterbacks*, p. 109.

Chapter 5: Joe Namath: The Symbol

56. Quoted in Charles Moritz, ed., *Current Biography Yearbook: 1966*. New York: H.W. Wilson, 1966, p. 291.

57. Quoted in Leigh Montville, "Off Broadway Joe," *Sports Illustrated*, July 14, 1997, p. 81.

58. Quoted in Phil Berger, *Joe Namath: Maverick Quarterback*. New York: Cowles, 1969, p. 6.

59. Quoted in "The Crimson Tide," *CBS Sportsline*. www.cbs.sportsline.com.

60. Quoted in Moritz, *Current Biography Yearbook: 1966*, p. 292.

61. Quoted in "Football's Super Star: Joseph William Namath," *New York Times*, January 13, 1969.

62. Quoted in Herskowitz, *The Quarterbacks*, p. 63.

63. Quoted in Moritz, *Current Biography Yearbook: 1966*, p. 293.

64. Quoted in Larry Schwartz, "Namath Was a Lovable Rogue," *ESPN*. www.espn.go.com.

65. Quoted in Herskowitz, *The Quarterbacks*, p. 67.

66. Quoted in Herskowitz, *The Quarterbacks*, p. 62.

Chapter 6: Joe Montana: The Coolest
67. Quoted in King, *Football*, p. 112.

68. Quoted in Larry Schwartz, "Montana Was Comeback King," *ESPN*. www.espn.go.com.

69. Joe Montana and Bob Raissman, *Audibles: My Life in Football*. New York: Avon Books, 1986, p. 1.

70. Quoted in Charles Moritz, ed., *Current Biography Yearbook: 1983*. New York: H.W. Wilson, 1983, p. 251.

71. Quoted in Glenn Dickey, "Bill Walsh's Big Role in Montana's Greatness," *San Francisco Chronicle*, December 16, 1997.

72. Quoted in Dickey, "Bill Walsh's Big Role in Montana's Greatness."

73. Quoted in Dickey, "Bill Walsh's Big Role in Montana's Greatness."

74. Quoted in Dickey, "Bill Walsh's Big Role in Montana's Greatness."

75. Quoted in Moritz, *Current Biography Yearbook: 1983*, p. 252.

76. Quoted in Jonathan Curiel, "Super Four," *San Francisco Chronicle*, December 15, 1997.

77. Quoted in Herskowitz, *The Quarterbacks*, p. 306.

78. Quoted in Herskowitz, *The Quarterbacks*, p. 306.

79. Quoted in Curiel, "Super Four."

80. Quoted in Mark Anderson, "Back in the Game: Montana Sets Up Camp," *Las Vegas Review-Journal*, September 22, 2002. www.lvrj.com.

81. Quoted in Schwartz, "Montana Was Comeback King."

Chapter 7: Dan Marino: The Arm
82. Quoted in Charles Moritz, ed., *Current Biography Yearbook: 1989*. New York: H.W. Wilson, 1989, p. 374.

83. Quoted in Larry Schwartz, "Marino's Golden Arm Changed Game," *ESPN*. www.espn.go.com.

84. Quoted in Moritz, *Current Biography Yearbook: 1989*, p. 375.

85. Quoted in *South Florida Sun-Sentinel*. www.sun-sentinel.com.

86. Quoted in Bob McCoy, ed., *The Sporting News Super Bowl Book—1987 Edition*. St. Louis, MO: Sporting News, 1987, p. 228.

87. Quoted in Schwartz, "Marino's Golden Arm Changed Game."

88. Quoted in Moritz, *Current Biography Yearbook: 1989*, p. 377.

89. Quoted in The Staff of Beckett Publications, *Beckett Great Sports Heroes: Dan Marino*. New York: House of Collectibles, 1996, p. 110.

90. Quoted in The Staff of Beckett Publications, *Beckett Great Sports Heroes*, p. 115.

91. Quoted in The Staff of Beckett Publications, *Beckett Great Sports Heroes*, p. 65.

92. Quoted in Peter King, "Letting Go," *Sports Illustrated*, March 20, 2000, p. 65.

93. Quoted in "Bristol University Discusses Dan the Man," *ESPN*. www.espn.go.com.

For Further Reading

Eddie Epstein, *Dominance*. Dulles, VA: Brassey's, 2002. This book takes an objective look at the best seasons of pro football's greatest teams.

Roland Lazenby, *The Pictorial History of Football*. San Diego, CA: Thunder Bay Press, 2002. Lazenby's work traces the long and colorful history of America's most popular spectator sport.

National Football League, *NFL's Greatest*. New York: DK, 2000. The Professional Football Hall of Fame Selection Committee picks the greatest players, teams, and games of all time.

National Football League, *NFL 2002 Record and Fact Book*. New York: Workman, 2002. The only record book authorized by the National Football League.

Don Weiss with Chuck Day, *The Making of the Super Bowl*. New York: McGraw-Hill, 2002. The untold saga of the creation and growth of sports' premier event, the Super Bowl.

WORKS CONSULTED

Phil Berger, *Joe Namath: Maverick Quarterback*. New York: Cowles, 1969. The biography of the flamboyant quarterback of the New York Jets.

Bob Carroll et al., eds., *Total Football*. New York: HarperCollins, 1997. Comprehensive football reference book containing statistics and historical essays.

Noel Epstein, ed., *Redskins: A History of Washington's Team*. Washington, DC: Washington Post Books, 1997. A history of the Washington Redskins through the eyes of the *Washington Post* sports staff.

Mickey Herskowitz, *The Quarterbacks*. New York: William Morrow, 1990. A look at some of the greats and near greats who have played the most difficult position in sports at the professional level.

Peter King, *Football: A History of the Professional Game*. New York: Time, 1996. A *Sports Illustrated* series volume that is an authoritative tribute to America's most popular sport.

———, *Greatest Quarterbacks*. New York: Time, 1999. A lavishly illustrated *Sports Illustrated* series volume that ranks the greatest quarterbacks of all time.

Jim Klobuchar and Fran Tarkenton, *Tarkenton*. New York: Harper and Row, 1976. The autobiography of the Minnesota Vikings' Hall of Fame quarterback.

Bob McCoy, ed., *The Sporting News Super Bowl Book—1987 Edition*. St. Louis, MO: Sporting News, 1987. The complete history of pro football's premier event.

Joe Montana and Bob Raissman, *Audibles: My Life in Football*. New York: Avon Books, 1986. Joe Montana's career in football in his own words.

Charles Moritz, ed., *Current Biography Yearbook: 1966*. New York: H.W. Wilson, 1966. Library volume that contains all of the biographies published in the *Current Biography* magazine in 1966.

———, *Current Biography Yearbook: 1969*. New York: H.W. Wilson, 1969. Library volume that contains all of the biographies published in the *Current Biography* magazine in 1969.

———, *Current Biography Yearbook: 1983*. New York: H.W. Wilson, 1983. Library volume that contains all of the biographies published in the *Current Biography* magazine in 1983.

———, *Current Biography Yearbook: 1989.* New York: H.W. Wilson, 1989. Library volume that contains all of the biographies published in the *Current Biography* magazine in 1989.

Walter Paulison, *The Tale of the Wildcats.* Chicago: Northwestern University Club of Chicago, 1951. A history of athletics at Northwestern University.

Beau Riffenburgh and David Boss, *Great Ones.* New York: Viking Penguin, 1989. Word and photographic portraits of the most famous men to have played football's most celebrated position.

The Staff of Beckett Publications, *Beckett Great Sports Heroes: Dan Marino.* New York: House of Collectibles, 1996. This volume in Beckett's Great Sports Heroes series examines the life of the greatest passer in NFL history.

Johnny Unitas and Ed Fitzgerald, *The Johnny Unitas Story.* New York: Grosset and Dunlap, 1968. The autobiography of the Baltimore Colts' all-time great quarterback.

Periodicals

"Baugh Suspects 1940 Redskins Threw Title Game to Spite Owner," *Amarillo Globe-News*, November 28, 1999.

Jonathan Curiel, "Super Four," *San Francisco Chronicle*, December 15, 1997.

Glenn Dickey, "Bill Walsh's Big Role in Montana's Greatness," *San Francisco Chronicle*, December 16, 1997.

"Football's Super Star: Joseph William Namath," *New York Times*, January 13, 1969.

"Graham's Legend Told Through Stories," *Mansfield News Journal*, November 4, 2002.

Peter King, "Letting Go," *Sports Illustrated*, March 20, 2000.

Leigh Montville, "Off Broadway Joe," *Sports Illustrated*, July 14, 1997.

Jan Reid, "Legends of the Fall," *Texas Monthly*, November 1997.

Dennis Tuttle, "Still Slingin'," *Sporting News*, November 7, 1994.

Mark Wilson, "Baugh: 'Really, Baseball Was My Best Sport,'" *Abilene Reporter-News*, April 25, 2002.

Paul Zimmerman, "Revolutionaries," *Sports Illustrated*, August 17, 1998.

Internet Sources

Mark Anderson, "Back in the Game: Montana Sets Up Camp," *Las Vegas Review-Journal*, September 22, 2002. www.lvrj.com.

"Bristol University Discusses Dan the Man," *ESPN*. www.espn.go.com.

Bob Carter, "Unitas Surprised Them All," *ESPN*. www.espn.go.com.

"The Crimson Tide," *CBS Sportsline*. www.cbs.sportsline.com.

Andy Friedlander, "Sammy Baugh," *Dallas-Fort Worth Star Telegram*, September 29, 2002. www.drw.com.

Shane Hannon, "Legends: Fran Tarkenton," *Online Athens*. www.onlineathens.com.

John McFarland, "Hall of Famer Sammy Baugh Reflects Fifty Years After Career Ended," *Yahoo!* www.ca.yahoo.com.

"One Hundred Greatest Players of All-Time: Number Three Sammy Baugh," *College Football News*. www.collegefootballnews.com.

"Otto Graham: He Was the Man," *NFL History Network*. www. nflhistory.net.

Larry Schwartz, "'Automatic Otto' Defined Versatility," *ESPN*. www.espn.go.com.

———, "Baugh Perfected the Perfect Pass," *ESPN*. www.espn. go.com.

———, "Marino's Golden Arm Changed Game," *ESPN*. www.espn. go.com.

———, "Montana Was Comeback King," *ESPN*. www.espn.go.com.

———, "Namath Was a Lovable Rogue," *ESPN*. www.espn.go.com.

"Unitas Dies of Heart Attack at Sixty-Nine," *NFL*. www.nfl.com.

"Unitas' Star Rose After Yankee Stadium Heroics," *ESPN*. www. espn.co.com.

"Unitas Was Original, Incredible," *NFL*. www.nfl.com.

Websites

Georgia Dogs (www.georgiadogs.ocsn.com). The official site of the University of Georgia Bulldogs.

South Florida Sun-Sentinel (www.sun-sentinel.com). Site of the South Florida Sun-Sentinel newspaper.

PICTURE CREDITS

ABOUT THE AUTHOR

John F. Grabowski is a native of Brooklyn, New York. He holds a bachelor's degree in psychology from City College of New York and a master's degree in educational psychology from Teacher's College, Columbia University. He has been a teacher for thirty-three years, as well as a freelance writer, specializing in the fields of sports, education, and comedy. His body of published work includes forty-three books; a nationally syndicated sports column; consultation on several math textbooks; articles for newspapers, magazines, and the programs of professional sports teams; and comedy material sold to Jay Leno, Joan Rivers, Yakov Smirnoff, and numerous other comics. He and his wife, Patricia, live in Staten Island with their daughter, Elizabeth.

UPSIDE-DOWN DOGS

UPSIDE-DOWN DOGS

SERENA HODSON

St. Martin's Griffin
New York

www.stmartins.com

The Library of Congress Cataloging-in-Publication Data is available upon request.

ISBN 978-1-250-13111-9 (paper over board)
ISBN 978-1-250-13112-6 (e-book)

Our books may be purchased in bulk for promotional, educational, or business use. Please contact your local
bookseller or the Macmillan Corporate and Premium Sales Department at 1-800-221-7945, extension 5442, or by
e-mail at MacmillanSpecialMarkets@macmillan.com.

First Edition: October 2017

10 9 8 7 6 5 4 3 2 1

To Rocco, Ralph, Henri, Simon, and Garfunkel. This book was created out of the joy you showed me from behind a lens. Thank you for your patience with me and my camera. I'm forever in your debt.

Your loving human

ACKNOWLEDGMENTS

Creating this book has been the most magical experience, and I am forever grateful for the people who have helped me make this dream come true.

My first and most enormous thank-you is to my kind and ever so patient husband, Neil Southwell. Thank you for giving me continuous support, guidance, love, and encouragement. I could not have done this without you by my side. Thank you to Merrin McCormick and your amazing lady brains. You are a true and wonderful friend who I cherish dearly. I am forever grateful for your selfless support and guidance to see my work get published. And a huge thank-you to Alicia Adamopoulos for your constant encouragement, advice, and most of all—believing in me. You have the biggest heart and are someone I treasure dearly. To Wendy Walklate, my team leader, thank you for your support, endless encouragement and believing in me. Thank you for always being there to listen and pick me up when I fall and lose my way. And a big thank-you to Michelle Tessler for believing in *Upside-Down Dogs* and helping me achieve a dream of being published. I'm forever grateful to you. To St. Martin's Press and my forever patient editor, Daniela Rapp. Thank you for seeing the vision of *Upside-Down Dogs*. Your quick responsive support and your enthusiasm for this book have been undoubtedly appreciated. And, of course, a thousand thanks to all the dog owners who allowed me to photograph their treasured pets. This book could not have been made without your enthusiasm and patience with this project.

INTRODUCTION

When I first got involved in photography, I saw it as a hobby—a way for me to record those magical moments that happen in an animal's everyday life. At the time I was living with Rocco, my bull-mastiff, and my sister's dachshund, Ralph. Their relationship was my inspiration and what I managed to capture drove me to take my photography seriously. I've always been an animal lover, but I never knew that passion would lead to my life's purpose—photography. This creative outlet allows me to capture the joy dogs bring to my life and then share that with the world. I believe every animal has a secret life—a unique personality that few people get to witness. That's why I get so much satisfaction from capturing each individual animal's expression. I love working with animals because they have no hang-ups—they don't put on an act, they don't complain about an unflattering photo and most of all, they make me happy. My aim is to capture the unique personality and humor that animals can bring into our lives. I believe a home isn't complete without a companion animal.

This book began with a simple idea—to capture the delight and joy of dogs in an upside down pose. Their facial expressions offer an antidote to human stress that should be bottled and sold as medication. My two bulldogs, Simon and Garfunkel, make me laugh every day—they keep me grounded through stressful times and always improve my mood with their antics and attitudes to life. We live complicated lives and we often dwell on the downside of situations—that's why we need dogs. Simon and Garfunkel are my best friends because they bring an optimistic and fun-loving perspective to every day. A ride in the car is like a roller-coaster ride, a bowl of kibble is a delicious five-star meal, and rolling around on their backs is heaven on earth for them. This is where I saw my first glimpse of *Upside-Down Dogs* captured in that unique moment of on-bed-upside-down-bliss. Through my dogs' eyes I can see life's silver linings and find an upside to getting out of bed every day, no matter what, and I thought this inspiration needed to be shared. This project goes to the heart of why humans and dogs have such a wonderful, symbiotic relationship. We need dogs to help us find joy in everyday pleasures, and our dogs need us to make the bed so they can jump up and roll around.

UPSIDE-DOWN DOGS

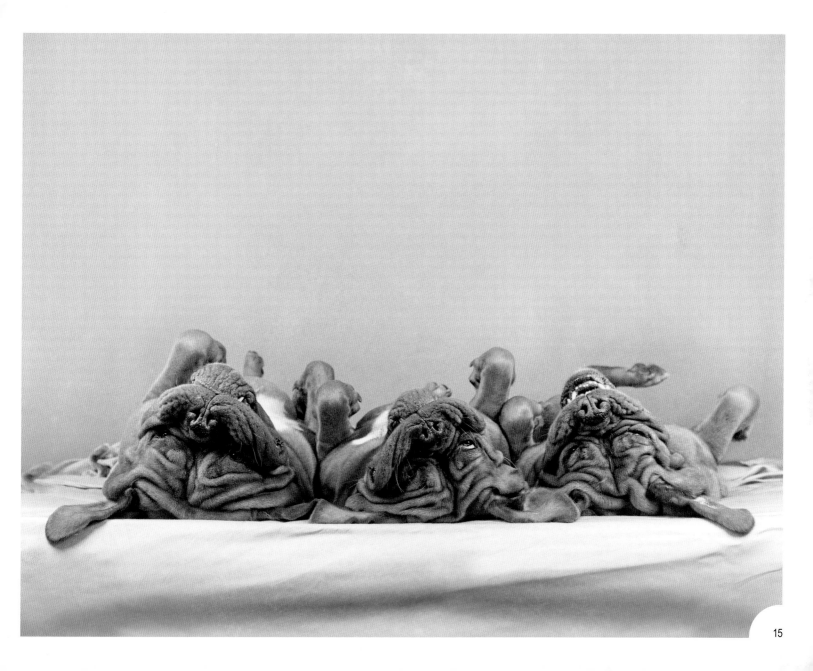

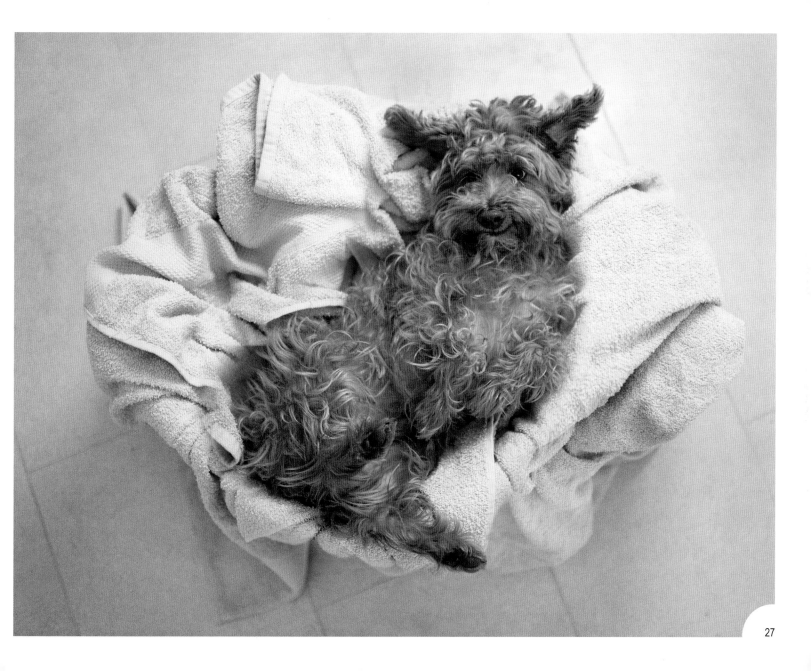

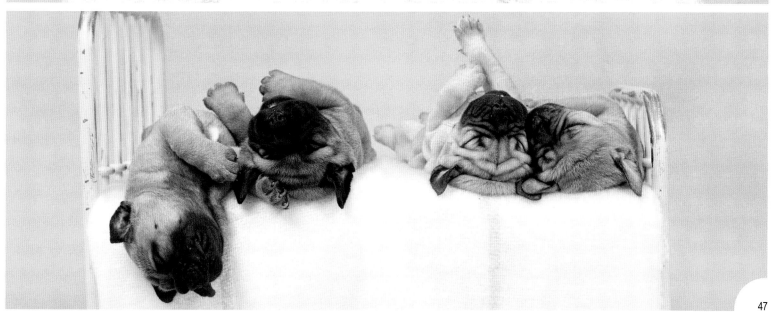

47

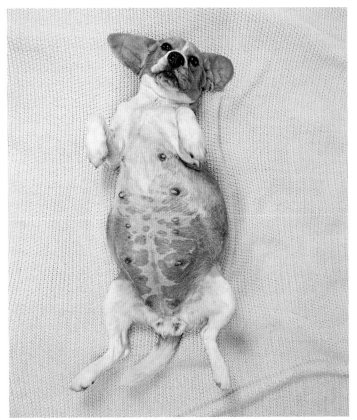

73

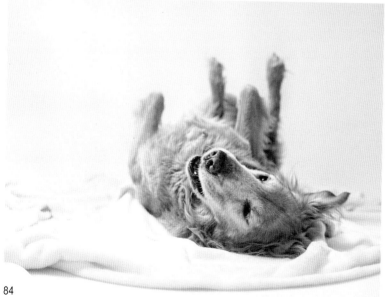

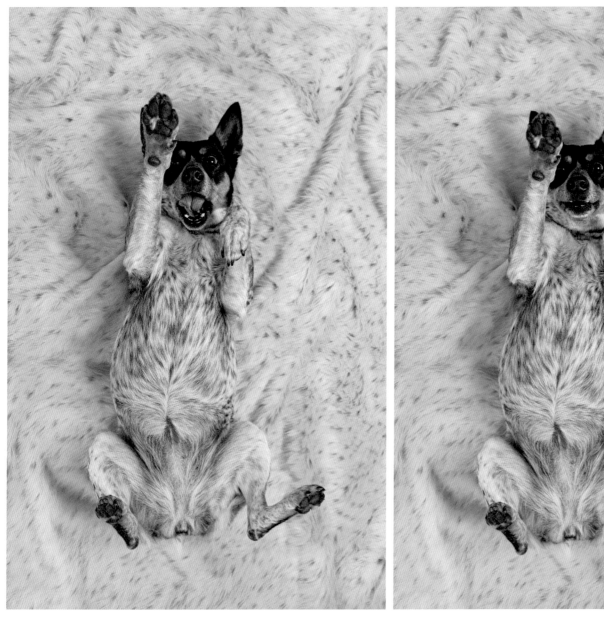

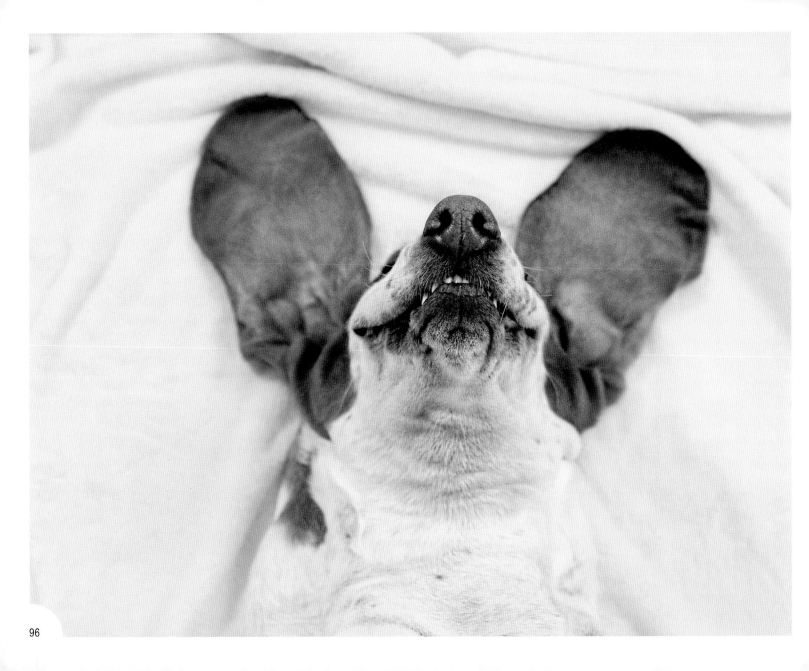

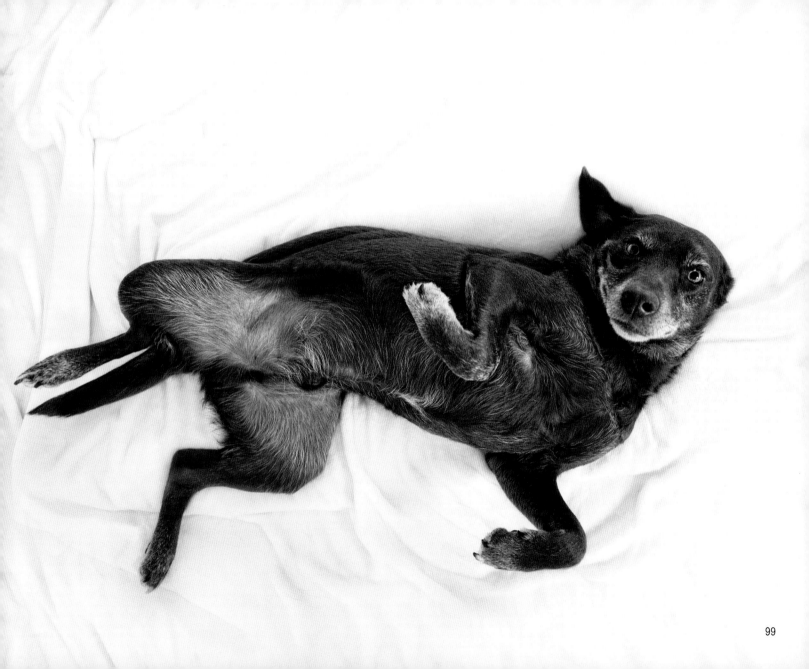

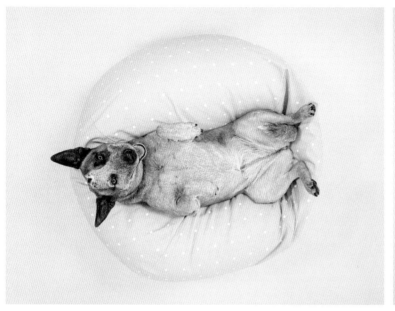

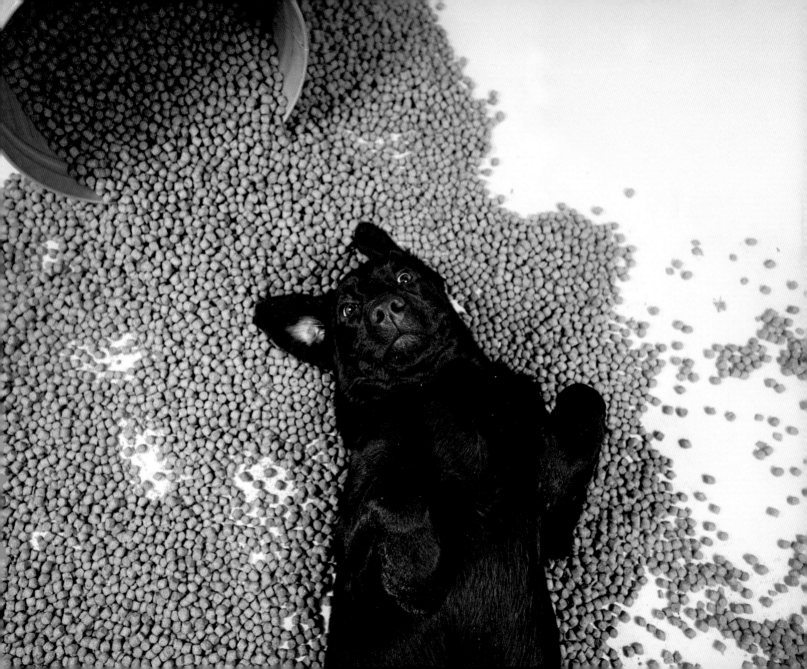